CW00497052

Travellers

GOA AND KERALA

BY
ANIL MULCHANDANI

Produced by
Thomas Cook Publishing

Written by Anil Mulchandani

Original photography by CPA Media

Original design by Laburnum Technologies Pvt Ltd

Editing and page layout by Cambridge Publishing Management Limited, 149B Histon Road, Cambridge CB4 3JD
Series Editor: Clare Ranson

Published by Thomas Cook Publishing
A division of Thomas Cook Tour Operations Limited

PO Box 227, The Thomas Cook Business Park, Unit 15/16, Coningsby Road, Peterborough PE3 8SB, United Kingdom
E-mail: books@thomascook.com
www.thomascookpublishing.com

ISBN:1-841573-87-6

Head of Thomas Cook Publishing: Donald Greig
Project Editor: Charlotte Christensen
Project Administration: Michelle Warrington
DTP: Steven Collins

Printed and bound in Spain by: Grafo Industrias Gráficas, Basauri

Cover: Palolem Beach, prows of fishing boats. Photograph by Simon Reddy/Alamy
Inside cover: All photos by Brand X Pictures/Alamy, except bottom left by ImageGap/Alamy

CD manufacturing services provided by business interactive ltd, Rutland, UK
CD edited and designed by Laburnum Technologies Pvt Ltd.

Contents

Introduction

The states of Goa and Kerala run along the Arabian Sea coastline of India, rising eastward from the sea to the forested peaks of the Western Ghats. Justly famous for their fine beaches and lush vegetation, Goa and Kerala rank among India's most popular holiday destinations. Inland from the beaches are historic cities and towns, hill stations and wildlife sanctuaries that delight travellers.

Mother and child on Colva Beach

Isolated for centuries from the rest of India by their natural boundaries of hills and the sea, Goa and Kerala boast colourful temples, European-style churches and mosques that mirror the distinctive local cultures and international influences from centuries of global maritime contact. The traders, settlers and invaders brought with them their religions so that healthy Christian and Muslim populations balance the Hindu majority of the two states.

Temple architecture in Goa and Kerala is enchanting

While agriculture remains the mainstay of the economies of Goa and Kerala even today, with spices being an important export, tourism is a big earner for both the states. Recognising the importance of tourism, the state governments, together with private enterprise, have developed a sophisticated infrastructure that provides visitors with a multitude of possibilities. Sightseeing tours take visitors to churches, synagogues, mosques, palaces, impressive mansions, museums, and the forts that rise from the rocky outcrops of Goa and Kerala, offering scenic views of the coast. Travellers can explore the flea markets of Goa and the antique markets of Kerala. Even those with a minimal interest in wildlife will enjoy visiting the tiger reserves and elephant sanctuaries of Kerala or viewing Goa's state animal, the gaur (Indian bison), at Bhagwan Mahaveer Sanctuary.

Houseboat cruises are a unique way to tour the villages along the backwaters of Kerala, while in Goa, boat trips provide a great way to view dolphins, crocodiles and coastal birds along the waterways. All this is balanced by wide-ranging accommodation facilities from forts and mansions converted into heritage hotels, to contemporary holiday resorts and business hotels that ensure a comfortable stay.

But, above all, travellers remember Goa and Kerala for their smiling people and laid-back charm that makes them want to return time and time again for the kind of relaxing holiday that is rare in India.

Thomas Cook was selling steamer tickets to India by 1870. In 1873, Thomas Cook himself visited India during a world tour and visited the Temperance Society of the Agra Garisson and promised to sponsor a library so that they would not return to drinking. By the 1880s, the company was organising guided tours in India and offering tours for Indian residents to other countries. In 1887, Thomas Cook advertised a wide range of itineraries and by 1891, the company had set up its first banking service in India; a year later, pamphlets with practical information were being published. Today, Thomas Cook has offices and banking services in Goa and Kerala.

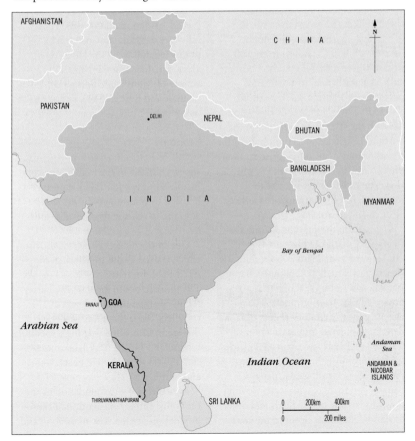

Goa: Land and People

The former Portuguese enclave of Goa occupies a narrow strip of land between the Arabian Sea and the Western Ghats. It owes much of its fame to the coastline that forms the western boundary of the state. Besides beach tourism, which is an important source of revenue for the state, parts of the coast, called *khazans*, have also been developed for shipping, fisheries and salt production.

The children of fishermen learning the trade

Geography

Goa is one of India's smallest states, about 100km (62 miles) from north to south along the coast, and rarely exceeding 60km (37 miles) from west to east, where it shares common borders with Maharashtra to its north and northeast and Karnataka to its south and southeast. A number of rivers flow through the state from Terakhol in the north to Galgibaga in the south, with the Mandovi and Zuari estuaries separating the two districts of North and South Goa. The estuaries are lined with mangrove forests that support a variety of birds and marine life.

Rising from the coast and along the rivers are the laterite plateaux that jut out seaward as headlands, providing the sites for forts such as Terakhol, Chapora, Aguada and Cabo De Rama that protected Goa from invaders. The laterite plateaux comprise most of Goa's densely populated midlands where terraced orchards and plantations grow spices, coconut palms and fruits like pineapple, jackfruit, guava, papaya, banana and mango, with water flowing down to irrigate paddy fields and other lowland cultivation closer to the coast.

In the east are the Sahyadri ranges of the Western Ghats where the peaks exceed 1,100m (3,609ft) high. These hilly areas are among Goa's least populated and most thickly forested areas. The forests are inhabited by a variety of wildlife, including sloth bear, panther and gaur (*see p4*), and are a paradise for birdwatchers.

Economy

Goa is one of India's most prosperous states, with one of the highest per-capita incomes in the country, its economy boosted by remittances from Goans working in other states of India and overseas.

One of the biggest earners is tourism, which started in the 1960s when hippies discovered the charm of Goa's beaches. The tourism boom grew when charter flights brought in plane-loads of travellers. Since then, tourism has thrived in Goa, attracting high-spending foreign and Indian travellers to its five-star and boutique hotels, beach resorts and heritage hotels.

Agriculture is the foundation of the economy, employing about half the population of Goa. The main food and cash crops are rice, maize, oilseeds, sugarcane, cashew nuts, spices, rubber, fruits, vegetables and garden plants. Large irrigation projects have been implemented to increase agricultural production. Goa also has a sizable number of people reliant on fishing for their livelihood.

There are a number of small and medium-sized industrial units, especially those that make use of the state's natural resources, such as food processing and canning units. Iron ore and other minerals are major exports of Goa, and mining continues despite opposition from the environmental lobby.

Today, the government is encouraging investment and infrastructure development in other sectors, with a particular focus on information technology.

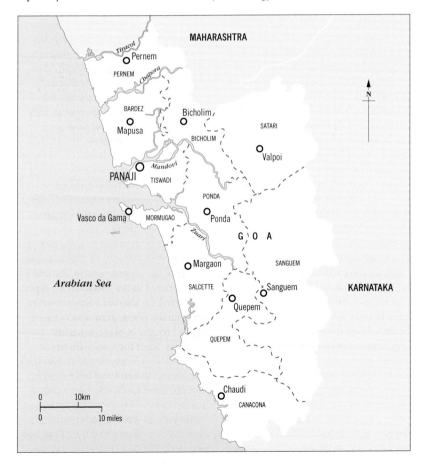

History

321–184 BC	Goa is part of the Kuntala administrative area under the Maurya Dynasty, the major power in India.
2nd century AD	The Bhoj Dynasty rules from Chandrapur, near the present village of Chandor.
6th–10th centuries	The Chalukyas of Badami rule Goa with the local Kadambas as their feudatories.
11th century	The Kadambas build the new port of Goppakapatna or Govepuri (Gove), ideally suited to benefit from maritime trade. Trade with Zanzibar and Sri Lanka flourishes and ties are strengthened with Arab traders.
14th century	Islamic invasions disrupt Goa. Gove is destroyed and Muhamad Tuglaq's army level Chandrapur. The Muslims of the Deccan form the Bahmani Dynasty and take control of Goa. In 1378 the Hindu Vijayanagar Dynasty emerges victorious over the Bahmani Dynasty and Goa becomes part of their kingdom headquartered at Hampi. Trade thrives under the Vijayanagar Dynasty, especially the export of spices and the import of Arabian horses.
1469	The Bahmanis, under Muhamad Shah, capture Goa. They destroy the old capital of Govepuri and establish a new city, Gove, now known as Old Goa.
1489	The Bahmanis divide into factions. Yusuf Ali Khan, who established the Bijapur Sultanate, inherits Goa. He makes Gove his second capital and establishes a fort on the River Mandovi in the area that is now Panaji. Trade flourishes and Goa becomes an embarkation point for pilgrimages to Mecca.
1510	Alfonso de Albuquerque attacks Goa in March and takes it successfully from the Adil Shah Sultan but loses it again a few months later. After the monsoon, Alfonso de Albuquerque attacks Goa again and takes it on St Catherine's day, 25th November. He massacres Muslims who had supported the sultan and gives powers to Hindus.

1542	St Francis Xavier arrives in Goa.		remains until 1813, despite Portuguese protests.
1560	The Inquisition begins ushering in a period of dissent. Hindus and Muslims alike are attacked in the areas of the 'Old Conquest'. Hindus are forbidden from practising their religion and even Christians live in fear because of the repression of orders.	**1821**	Goa is allocated representation in Lisbon's Parliament.
		1843	Panaji is officially declared the capital of Goa.
		1881	The first ever railway links are established between Mormugoa and the peninsula of India.
17th century	The Dutch attack Goa and take Cochin. Marathas attack Goa later in the century but move back following the threat of Mughal attacks on their territory.	**1905**	Goa's first mines are opened.
		1928	The Goa Congress Party is formed.
		1949	India becomes independent from British rule.
1737–9	Marathas attack Goa and take parts of North and South Goa. Settlement is reached between the Portuguese and the Marathas.	**19 Dec 1961**	The Indian national government, under Prime Minister Jawaharlal Nehru, opposes Portuguese rule over Goa. In December 1961, the Indian army mounts Operation Vijay and the Indian government designates Goa a Union Territory.
1774	Edicts ban the Inquisition.		
1781–91	The Portuguese make new conquests in Goa.		
1787	The Pinto Revolt takes place, in which Goan churchmen ask for equal rights.	**30 May 1987**	Goa receives statehood.
1797	The British occupy Goa, and the British Garrison	**1988–2004**	*See pp10–11 for recent political developments in Goa.*

Governance

India has sustained a constitutional democratic system based on secularism, equal rights for women, universal suffrage, human rights and a ban on untouchability, for more than 50 years, despite tremendous challenges. There were, however, two years when prime minister Indira Gandhi imposed a ban on political activity as an emergency measure.

The old methods of tilling fields are still practised

Government of India
India is a sovereign democratic republic, and all citizens over 18 years of age are eligible to vote. The president is the official head, but exercises his powers under the authority of the prime minister and with the advice of the council of ministers who are selected by the prime minister.

There are two houses of parliament. The lower house, *Lok Sabha* or council of people, comprises members elected by the constituencies of the country and two nominated members of the Anglo-Indian community. Of the 543 elected seats of the *Lok Sabha*, 125 are reserved for scheduled tribes and undereducated classes. The upper house, *Rajya Sabha* or council of states, has 12 members nominated by the president and 233 members elected by the state assemblies.

The 29 states have legislative assemblies with the governor as the official head, nominated by the president and the chief minister. The governor is responsible for the actual administration of the state with the cabinet of ministers. Like the central government, most of the states have two houses of parliament – the *Rajya Sabha* comprising mainly nominated members and the *Vidhan Sabha* consisting of the elected members.

There is a clear line of distinction between the role of central and state governments. The central government controls the armed forces, aviation, railways, postal services, currency and international affairs. The state governments are responsible for industry, agriculture, roads, forestry and environment, and internal security.

The political scene in India
The Congress Party has been a dominant force in the politics of India since 1885 when it was established as the first Indian national political institution. Jawaharlal Nehru became the first prime minister of India in 1947, and Congress won seven of the first ten general elections held in India. At the 11th general elections in 1996, Congress was defeated by the *Bharatiya Janta Party* (BJP). A coalition was formed, called the United Front, but it fell in 1998 when Congress withdrew support and the BJP came to power with Atal Behari Vajpayee as the prime minister. BJP won the elections in 1999 and Vajpayee once more became prime minister of India.

Goan government and politics

Goa was a union territory administered by the president of India until 1987 when it was given full statehood. It has a 40-member legislative assembly, with two seats in the *Lok Sabha* and one in the *Rajya Sabha*.

Congress won most of the elections in Goa, but regional issues, such as the role of *Marathi* as a language, and the environment, are still key. The BJP defeated Congress in the 1999 elections and Jaochim Alemao became one of the first non-Catholic representatives of Mormugoa constituency in the *Lok Sabha*. In 2001 BJP took over the state administration, with Manohar Parriker as the chief minister.

Political party rallies in Goa are vibrant occasions

Culture

In spite of 451 years of Portuguese rule, Goa retains most of its earlier cultural traditions. The Portuguese may have introduced Christianity to Goa, but even the local Catholic population follows a caste system similar to that of the Hindus. Christians, Hindus and Muslims recognise and participate in each other's religious festivals, and this contributes to Goa's relaxed atmosphere.

Kathakali performances are renown in southern India

Caste

The Hindus follow a caste system that has to some extent spread to other religions. The four main castes are *Brahmin* (the priestly caste), *Kshatriya* (the warrior caste), *Vaishya* (the trading community) and *Sudra* (the agricultural caste). These castes are hereditary and have no relation to the occupation or financial status of the person today. The Saraswat, Padhya, Bhatt, Kramavant and Chitpavans are among the priestly group of *Brahmins*, while artisans like goldsmiths are called *Panchala Brahmins*.

Indigenous communities

The Kharvi Catholics claim to be the original inhabitants of Goa's coastal stretch. Descendants of Hindu fishing communities, they have accepted Portuguese names like Dias and D'Souza. The Thovois are Christian carpenters who provide furniture and woodcarvings to the churches of Goa.

The Kunbis, Velpis, Gawdes and Dangars are among the oldest communities of Goa; while many of them have joined the mainstream, some Kunbis and Velpis still live in traditional thatch-roofed houses, herding livestock on the southern hillsides and following ancestral worship rituals. Traditionally, Kunbi women wear copper bangles on their arms, bead necklaces, and oiled hair tied into distinctive coils. The Lambanis from Karnataka visit Goa to sell their wares at Mapusa Market and Anjuna Flea Market.

Music and dance

Goans are known in India and abroad for their love of music and dance. With their long exposure to European influences, Goan musicians are in great demand for westernised music and dance performances that are the rage in India today.

The most typical dance of Goa is the *mando*, a Konkani love song accompanied by a stringed instrument like the violin and a percussive instrument like the local terracotta drum. The men and women dance in two rows, the men carrying colourful hankies and the women sporting fans. Other dances of Goa are the Portuguese-style *corradinho*, martial dances such as *ghode modni*, Hindu *dhalo* and *fugdi* dances, the harvest dance called *gof*, and the percussive stick dance called *tonyamell*. Local street plays, called *tiatr*, are usually performed in the Konkani language.

Language

The official language of Goa is Konkani, written in the Devanagri script, and it has been the medium of instruction at schools from 1991. Marathi is also widely spoken and taught. Only a few Goans still consider Portuguese their second language, but English has recently become a popular medium of instruction. The national language, Hindi, is taught as a second language in school.

A tribal woman sells her wares at Anjuna flea market

Religion

With its many churches and its colonial history, Goa gives first-time visitors the impression that it is a Christian majority state, but in fact the majority of Goans follow Hinduism. Christians are the largest minority, and there is a small population of Muslims, while Jews, Parsees, Jains, Buddhists and Sikhs make up the rest of the population.

Ganesh, the elephant-headed deity

Hinduism

Hinduism is a religious tradition with ancient roots dating back to the third and second millennia BC. With no founder, prophet or church-like organisation to define the rules, Hinduism has embraced new features and a diversity of religious beliefs even until recent times. The holy books of the Hindus are the *Vedas* (incorporating the *Upanishads* as the final volumes), which are often considered the foundation of Indian philosophy, with epics like the *Ramayana* and *Mahabharata*, and the *Bhagavadgita* which is based on the philosophies of Lord Krishna as they

Hindu shrines are dedicated to particular deities and are important places of *puja* – ritualistic worship

were related to warrior prince Arjun in an episode of the *Mahabharata*.

Hindus believe in a cycle of reincarnation determined by their *karma*, the consequences of former actions that can flow into the next life. The aims of a Hindu are to attain material wealth honestly (*artha*), satisfy all desires (*kama*) and perform all duties (*dharma*), all of which will lead, through good *karma*, to *moksha*, liberation from the endless rebirth cycle.

An aspect of Hinduism that most visitors to India find hard to understand is the multitude of gods and goddesses. Actually, most of them are incarnations and manifestations of a few, and this may be the result of Hinduism incorporating regional beliefs into its pantheon. Three Gods are considered integral to Hinduism: Brahma as the creator, Vishnu as the preserver of the universe (usually worshipped as one of his many incarnations that rid the world of destroying forces like demons) and Shiva, the destroyer, who is worshipped in many forms, such as Natraja when he dances to destroy evil. The consort of Brahma is Sarasvati, the goddess of learning. Vishnu's consort Lakshmi is worshipped as the goddess of wealth, and Shiva's consort Parvati has many manifestations, including Durga and Kali, goddesses of power and destruction. Most Hindus start a new venture by worshipping Ganesh, the elephant-headed son of Lord Shiva, who is said to bring luck, knowledge and prosperity.

Some key features of Hindu religious traditions are *darshan* ('to see'), which denotes the importance of visiting holy places, *puja* or ritualistic worship, and cremation of the dead.

An interesting Hindu tradition in Goa is the reverence of the basil plant (*tulsi*) that is grown outside temples and most Goan Hindu houses.

Christianity

The Portuguese introduced Roman Catholicism to Goa soon after their arrival in 1510. Since then, most Goan Christians belong to the Roman Catholic Church, one of the world's largest Christian groups tracing descent from the Western Catholic Church. They acknowledge the authority of the Pope, whose utterances are considered binding.

Pope Clement VII erected the See of Goa on January 31, 1933, with a wide-ranging jurisdiction. St Francis Xavier, a Jesuit, arrived here in 1542 and administered to the Goan Christians.

Hindu temples are a feast for the eyes both internally and externally

background

You will see an abundance of religious symbols around Goa

The Jesuits established the first printing press in India and published their works in vernacular languages.

On 1557 Goa was made an Archbishopric, with suffragans (assistant bishops) in other parts of India. In 1572, Pope Gregory XIII, in his *Brief*, dated March 15, acknowledged the Archbishop of Goa as the Primate of the East. From 1928, this Archdiocese is known as 'Goa and Daman'.

The Portuguese instigated harsh policies to impose Catholic orthodoxy on the people of Goa. A tribunal called the Goa Inquisition was set up in 1560: Hinduism was banned and Christians lived in fear. The Inquisition met regularly and held great public trials, with execution of those they believed were infidels. Punishment ranged from stripping the victims of their possessions or detaining them in dungeons to public strangling and even burning at the stake. Later centuries saw the suppression of religious orders, with the Jesuits banned in 1759.

Islam
See pp72–3.

Buddhism
Ancient cave sites confirm that Goa was once inhabited by Buddhists, but the religion did not survive in the state. Today, the Buddhists of Goa are recent settlers, such as the Tibetans. Buddhism is based on the beliefs of Sidhartha Gautama Buddha who was born into a princely family in the 6th century BC. His preaching is often regarded as a reaction to Hinduism, accepting the doctrine of reincarnation and the law of *karma*, but rejecting the concept of a pantheon of gods and the caste system.

Jainism
Like the Buddhists, the Jains in Goa are immigrants from other states like Gujarat and Rajasthan, although the forests of Bicholim and Satari are said to have been refuges of Jains and Buddhists from resurgent Hinduism and Islamic invasions. There are a few Jain temples

in Goa, most of them recent. The key features of the Jain religion are liberation from the wheel of rebirth and the belief that all life is sacred. Strict vegetarianism is a feature of Jainism, for Jains believe that even the smallest life form has a soul.

Zoroastrianism

The Zoroastrians came to India in the 8th century, landing on the Gujarat coast from the Persian Gulf, and are known as Parsees. Parsees trace their belief back to Zoroaster, an Iranian prophet of the 6th or 7th century BC, and their holy book is the *Avesta*.

Zoroastrians believe in one god, Ahura Mazda, seen as rejecting evil for good and purifying thought, word and action. The focal point for Zoroastrian worship is the fire from ancient times, and earth and air are also considered sacred.

Judaism
See pp72–3.

One of many Christian shrines in Old Goa

Festivals

Most Hindu, Christian and Muslim festivals are well observed in Goa, with the intermingling of religious communities being a special feature of the ceremonies. Hindu and Muslim festivals follow the lunar calendar, which differs from the western calendar, and dates can be checked with the tourist offices in Goa.

Ganesh Chaturthi is a popular annual event

Feast of the Three Kings
6 January
This festival is celebrated with re-enactments of the three kings bringing gifts for Jesus Christ. The best places to witness the celebrations are Chandor, Cansaulim, and Reis Magos where a large fair is held at the 16th-century church.

Mahashivratri
February/March
This is a Hindu festival commemorating the night when Lord Shiva danced the Tandav, the dance of destruction, with ceremonies at Arvelam, Fatorpa, Mangesh, Nangesh, Queula and Shiroda temples.

Carnival
February/March
Celebrating the arrival of spring, the Carnival takes place shortly before the start of Lent. A non-religious event, it is a good time to see Goans in full celebratory mode. The event is opened by a Goan appointed as the life of the party and playing the part of King Momo (King of Misrule), who makes a decree ordering his 'subjects' to forget their worries and have a good time. On *Sabada Gordo* (Fat Saturday), he leads a colourful procession of floats through

the streets, with depictions of Goan folk culture and contemporary messages, musicians, people dancing the *Mando* and competing teams in flamboyant costumes. Carnival is one big party, the revelry lasting for three days, with dance parties at clubs and hotels.

Shigmotsav
March
Shigmo marks the climax of spring, with pageants of fanciful floats and musicians playing percussive instruments. People have fun throwing coloured paint and water at each other. The festivities are best witnessed at Panaji, Margao, Vasco da Gama and Mapusa.

The Procession of All Saints
March
On the Monday of Holy Week each year there is a procession of floats featuring life-size statues of saints from St Andrew's Church at Goa Velha. The procession takes a loop from the church through the Goa Velha village and ends at the church square for a candlelit service. The saints' statues can be viewed for two days after the procession. This is the only procession of its kind outside Rome, and the tradition dates to the

17th century. The local fair offers good opportunities to buy handicrafts.

Feast of Our Lady of Miracles
March/April
Held 16 days after Easter, this festival is celebrated by large numbers of Hindus and Christians, who gather to venerate the image of Nossa Senhora de Milagres and to celebrate the feast day of the Sabin, on which a huge fair and market are held at Mapusa.

Ganesh Chaturthi
August/September
Lord Ganesh is venerated during this festival, which is one of the most popular Hindu events in Goa. On the last day the idols of Ganesh are paraded in a procession, accompanied by loud music, before immersion in the sea or at one of the rivers or inland lakes.

Christmas
25 December
As elsewhere, Christmas in Goa is the day for family gatherings, feasting and celebrations, and special sweets are prepared. The midnight Mass at Goa is called 'Cock Crow' because it traditionally goes on until the early hours of the morning.

Goan women adorn their hair with flowers during festival times

Architecture

As a legacy of its unusual colonial history, Goa's architecture incorporates local and international influences. While the churches are Indian versions of European architecture, the temples integrate Muslim and European architecture into a traditional Hindu layout.

A typical Goan temple tower

Churches

Churches are a dominant feature of Goa's landscape. They are usually positioned on hilltops or in the main squares of villages and towns. Generally constructed in European style, Goa's churches are distinguished by the rich heritage of Indian craftsmanship, which is evident even in the Church of Our Lady of Rosary, the oldest surviving church in Goa. The churches are often cruciform in construction, with a sanctuary comprising the main altar and a richly ornamented backdrop called the reredos, a chancel with murals or woodcarvings, side altars and a long hall for the congregation. They are usually whitewashed to protect the laterite walls, and they have deep-set windows which are suited to Goa's climate.

Italian Renaissance and Baroque influences are evident in those churches built between 1550 and 1650, when the Portuguese undertook church-building activities with a missionary zeal. This period saw the building of two of Goa's best-known monuments, the Se Cathedral and the Basilica of Bom Jesus. Some of the churches, such as St Catejan Church of Old Goa, were entirely modelled on those of Rome.

The next hundred years saw the growth of the distinctive synthesis of Indian and Baroque architecture in churches like the Church of St Francis of Assisi, in Madgaon, Santana in Talaulim, and the churches of Divar Island. The artisans were given more freedom and decorated the churches with Indian motifs.

In the churches of the 18th century, Rococo features were incorporated into the design, and Indian artisans excelled in decorating the reredos, pulpits and vaulting of the chancels.

Temples

Goa has a number of Hindu temples built during the 18th and 19th centuries that have incorporated Christian and Muslim elements into traditional Hindu temple layouts of the porch, entrance hall, *mandapa* (hall) and *sanctum* (sanctuary). The *shikaras* (pyramidal towers with a bell-shaped section at the top), which are a feature of Hindu temples elsewhere, have been replaced in Goa by domes, *minarets* (slender towers with balconies) and East Indian roofs inspired by Mughal architecture. A unique feature of Goa's temples is the *deepasthamba*, or lamp tower, that looks like a column of light on festive occasions when lamps are lit in the niches of the towering structure.

Goan houses

In the 18th and 19th centuries, Goa's wealthy families commissioned houses in keeping with their wealth and status. Built like other Konkani houses, with laterite walls, Mangalore red-tiled roofs and inner courtyards, these houses were purpose-built to entertain guests, with an attractive reception hall and rooms for the balls and banquets that were a feature of the Goan lifestyle. The concept of functional rooms, such as libraries and studies, was introduced in the new houses, while large Baroque and Rococo windows, balconies and verandahs kept the interior cool. Taking advantage of trade ties, the owners imported marble and mosaic tiles, mirrors and glass from Europe, and porcelain and china from Macao. The Goan carpenters created beautiful rosewood and teak furniture for these houses, taking inspiration from imported pieces and designs.

The faithful queue to venerate the body of St Francis Xavier, Se Cathedral, Old Goa

Impressions

A popular tourist destination for many years, Goa is geared up for travellers and offers a variety of modern facilities not easily available in other states of India. A compact state by Indian standards, travellers find it easy to tour the beaches, towns and villages even during a short stay. The state capital, Panaji, is small enough for a visitor to walk around and see the main sights of the town.

Taking time to catch up on the news during a river ferry crossing

GETTING AROUND
Bus

Buses connect most towns and villages, and they are an economical and convenient way of getting around Goa, but they are often crowded and are not as comfortable as taxis. The state-owned Kadamba transport service has bus stations in the towns and stops at most villages. Ask at the bus station whether you need to buy tickets before getting on the bus at the counter or in the bus itself. Some buses have the option of a separate section for women travelling alone.

A road sign near Calangute

Private operators have attractive buses with comfortable seating to attract passengers, but often play loud music or videos. Most of these private buses connect Goa with Maharashtra and Karnataka.

Cars and taxis

Taxis are available at taxi stands in the main towns, outside popular hotels and resorts, at Dabolim Airport, Madgaon Railway Station, most bus terminals, and near tourist places. The drivers usually have a card with predetermined prices for transfers to towns and places of tourist interest. If you plan to visit lesser-known places, or want to retain the taxi for visiting more than one place, make sure you fix the price before setting off.

An alternative is to hire a car with a driver from a tour operator, hotel travel desk or the Goa Tourism Development Corporation. It is a good idea to hire a car for two or three days, which means you will be able to explore most of Goa's sights. The majority of drivers can speak English and act as interpreters, removing most of the usual hurdles that travellers face in India, such as asking for directions or accessing information.

They also help to interact with locals and the government offices. The rental is based on the number of hours, with a kilometre allowance. If you hire a car for more than a day, the night halt charge includes the driver's expenses, and he will expect a tip at the end of the tour.

Self-drive car hire is still in its infancy in India, although a few companies, such as Hertz, Wheels and Sai, do offer this service in Goa.

Cycling

Bicycles can be hired in most cities and towns of Goa. Indian cycles are heavy and do not have gears, but they are perfectly adequate for the flat coastal roads of Goa, and some operators now offer imported mountain bikes for hire. On the roadsides you will find repair shops that are nominally priced. Check the tyres and general condition of the cycle, and whether the bell and lights work. It may be a good idea to bring a light with you and a cord to strap down your baggage, as these are not easily available in India. Those travelling with children may find it necessary to bring a basket along or have one made. Do not leave your rucksack or any other baggage on the bicycle, as it could be an invitation to thieves.

If you bring your own bicycle with you, carry plenty of spares and a repair kit.

The streets of Goa are lined with auto-rickshaws eagerly awaiting their next passenger

Locals disembark from a Goan river ferry

Ferries

Although bridges have been built across the rivers of Goa, flat-bottomed ferries still operate to islands like Divar or across to places like Tiracol Fort in the far north of the state. The ferries are usually crowded with people, motor-cycles, scooters and cars. You can buy either a one-way or a return ticket.

Motorcycling

Motorbikes – ranging from 100cc to 350cc – can easily be hired in Goa. An alternative is the scooter, usually 100cc to 150cc, which has a lockable compartment for small items and a spare tyre on the back. Smaller mechanised bikes – mopeds – have no gears and are only suitable for short-distance travel.

It is a good idea to check the condition of the motorbike or scooter, and the documents (third-party insurance is compulsory in India), before hiring. An international driving licence is advisable.

Bring helmets with you, otherwise it may be necessary to buy them in Goa. Most travellers hiring motorbikes bring their own gloves, leathers, boots and other protective material. You can also ask the hotel travel desk for information about motorbike tour operators in Goa. Joining a tour can eliminate some of the hassles of hiring a motorbike and travelling in India.

Goa also has 'motorbike taxis' that are cheaper and faster than cars, but some insurance companies are known not to cover travellers for accidents on these.

Rickshaws

Auto-rickshaws are noisy and uncomfortable three-wheel vehicles with a driver in front and a bench or seats for two or more passengers. They are more economical than taxis and convenient for crowded and narrow streets because of their smaller size.

Trains

The Konkan Railway runs through Goa, with stations at Tiwim near the beaches of North Goa, Karmali near Old Goa and Panjim, Madgaon in Salcette and Cancona in the far south. However, train travel is not a very convenient way to get from one part of Goa to the other, unless you are staying at a hotel near one of the railway stations.

CULTURE SHOCK

India inevitably has a number of shocks for first-time visitors, particularly the crowds, poverty, dust and disease, but in a wealthy state like Goa, these social problems are restricted to a few areas. Although the people of Goa are used to

tourists, visitors from other states of India may stare, crowd around, giggle and involve you in inane conversation out of curiosity. Do not be surprised if strangers discuss personal matters, politics and religion with you, or ask questions about your family and income: Indians are openly curious and consider asking personal questions part of being warm and hospitable to visitors.

Bureaucratic hurdles, slow service, crowded roads and long queues can try your patience, but on the whole Goa is more relaxing and accustomed to looking after travellers than many other states in India are.

CONDUCT
Body language

In most of India, the customary greeting is to place the palms together as in prayer, and say *namaste*. Shaking hands is becoming more common, but only the most westernised Indians will shake hands with a woman. Indians use the right hand for eating and for social interactions like giving, receiving and shaking hands. It is polite to dress modestly away from the beaches, and most Indians do not smoke in front of seniors.

A motorbike made for two!

Try to seek your subjects' permission before taking photographs

Photography

Shooting photographs without asking permission is considered very rude in India, so you should always ask before you take photographs of local people, especially of women. On the other hand, children trying to edge their way into the frame, or curious people wanting to see your camera equipment could crowd you, so you need to be quite tolerant. Carry plenty of film and batteries, since it may prove hard to obtain the kind you need in Goa: for example, transparency film is not easily available.

Goa is sunny for most of the year, and slow film is ideal under these conditions, except during the monsoon months. There are many great opportunities to photograph 'picture-postcard' sunsets and lovely landscapes. Pack some fast film for cloudy days and for photography in the early morning and evening, especially if you plan to visit the wildlife reserves and forest areas. A UV filter may be useful for photography in bright light.

Camera thefts are common in India. Always take care of your camera, and do not leave it unattended in a hotel room or taxi.

Religious etiquette

Although India is a land of many religions, etiquette at most religious places is fairly standard. Visitors are expected to dress modestly and behave respectfully. You will have to take off your shoes and put out your cigarette before entering a temple or mosque. At mosques, you may have to cover your head, and women may not be allowed to enter during *namaz* (prayer times).

Women travellers

Goans are used to women tourists, but other Indian visitors may stare or make rude comments if they see western women in bathing clothes. Away from the beaches and swimming pools, women are expected to dress sensibly and not wear bikinis, swimsuits, shorts and skimpy skirts. Most Indian women do not drink or smoke.

It is advisable to observe local etiquette and dress modestly when entering religious areas

Panaji

Panaji (Panjim) is one of India's smallest and most pleasant state capitals, with attractive old quarters and a riverside boulevard. Its strategic location between the Mandovi river estuary and the hill of Altinho was recognised by Adil Shah, who built a fort palace at the site. This was the fort that Albuquerque's Portuguese forces had to overcome in order to capture Goa from the Sultan in 1510.

An old building in Panaji

Realising the strategic importance of Panaji, Albuquerque reinforced the fortifications and posted a garrison at the fort palace. It was merely a military outpost until 1634, when land was reclaimed to create a causeway between Old Goa and Panaji, and this proved to be a far-sighted move that subsequently led to the development of Panaji.

The Viceroy moved his residence to Panaji in 1754 and large-scale development took place in the 1820s and '30s, when streets, electricity and other civil services were developed. Eventually, Panaji became the capital of Goa by a Royal Decree of 1843, and retained its status after 1961 when the Government of India assumed control. Today, Panaji has administrative offices, shopping plazas, the Archbishop's residence, a port, and town planning in a grid formation with the main roads running parallel to the waterfront. *Panaji is 26km (16 miles) from Dabolim Airport and has good road connections to the railway stations of Goa.*

Church of Our Lady of the Immaculate Conception
Built in 1541, this church served as a landmark for the ship crews entering the Mandovi river estuary, and as a place to offer thanks for a safe landing. It was rebuilt in 1619 after becoming a parish church in 1600. Situated in a beautiful square of Panaji, a distinctive feature of the church is the impressive, four-tiered zigzag staircase, built in the 18th century when land was reclaimed in front of the building. Its arches were strengthened to bear the weight of the huge golden bell which was moved here in 1871 from St Augustine Church. Inside, the church has an altar to Our Lady of the Immaculate Conception, flanked by two ornate and heavily gilded altars to Jesus the Crucified and to Our Lady of the Rosary, with marble statues of St Paul and St Peter on either side.
Church Square, Jose Falcao Road, near Government of India Tourist Office, Panaji.

Idalcao Palace
This was the castle of the Sultan of Bijapur, Yusuf Adil Shah, whom the Portuguese called Idalcao. The building has been completely revamped, so it looks like a Portuguese colonial structure with sloping tiled roof and verandahs. It

became the Viceregal Palace from 1754 and the administrative hub of Panaji when the Viceroy moved residence to Cabo Rajniwas in 1918. After Goa became part of India in 1961, the Idalcao Palace was the first secretariat with the Indian Ashoka Chakra symbol replacing the Portuguese emblem. Today, it houses government offices.

In a small square near the Idalcao Palace is the statue of Abbe Faria, an 18th-century priest, in the process of hypnotising a woman.
Near the main boat terminus of Panaji.

Institute Menezes Braganza

This institute was established in 1871 to encourage literary and scientific interests among the people of Goa. Originally called Vasco da Gama Institute, it was renamed after Menezes Braganza, an important figure in Goa's struggle for freedom against the Portuguese. The entrance hall has blue tiles hand-painted by Jorge Calaco in 1935, set in a clockwise frieze depicting the mythical story of the Portuguese conquest of Goa. This leads to one of India's oldest public libraries, which houses a large collection of priceless books. Upstairs there's an art gallery exhibiting European and Goan paintings, rare prints and a table from the Inquisition.
Admission free Mon–Fri 9.30am–1pm & 2–5.45pm. Closed: public holidays.

The old colonial quarters

Fontainhas is an interesting old area of Panaji with terracotta-tiled houses set along narrow streets and climbing up Altinho hill. The houses are generally modest, with neoclassical façades and verandahs, and some have retained their ochre, yellow, blue and green coats of paint which date from the days when the Portuguese insisted that only churches could be painted white. The quarter takes its name from *Fonte*

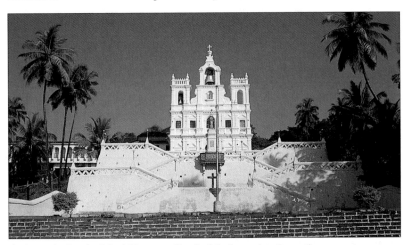

The impressive façade of the 16th century Church of the Immaculate Conception

Pheonix, a natural spring, and the water supply was further enhanced by a reservoir. The white-washed Chapel of St Sebastian has a crucifix that once hung in the Palace of the Inquisition, and then the Viceregal Palace, before it was brought here in 1812.

The adjoining old quarter is San Tome, named after the square where public executions took place during the 1843 Pinto Revolt (*see pp8–9*).
On the eastern promontory of the river.

PANAJI ENVIRONS
Cabo Rajniwas
This is the site of the great Portuguese Cabo fort, but only a section of the wall and some cannons are still standing. It was taken over by British troops from 1798 to 1813, and their cemetery can be seen from the access road. Today, it is the governor's residence and can only be visited for Mass at Our Lady of Cabo.

Goa Velha
This is one of the oldest conquests of the Portuguese, and it was an important port along the Zuari in Kadamba times. The port went into decline because it silted up, and it was destroyed by the Bahmani Muslims in 1470.

Today, Goa Velha is largely deserted, but the surrounding villages have some fine churches. The 18th-century Church of St Lawrence at Agassaim has a heavily gilded altar with a richly decorated Rococo reredos and a chancel with an

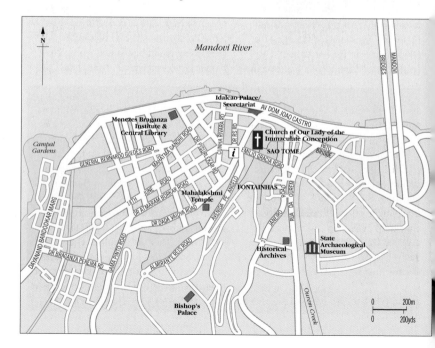

An example of the colonial architecture that dominates Panaji

attractive ceiling. Agassaim celebrates the Franciscan Procession of All Saints at St Andrew's Church.

The Pilar Seminary, a monastery established in 1613 by the Capuchin monks and named after the statue of Our Lady of Pilar which was brought from Spain, remains a centre of religious education. After the Capuchins were expelled from Goa in 1835, the Seminary and Our Lady of Pilar Church was taken over by Carmelites in 1858, who restored the abandoned buildings, and later it became the headquarters of the Missionary Society of St Xavier. The church has some interesting old statues, and the relatively recent chapel has lovely paintings. There is a museum here housing sculptures from an old Hindu temple that stood at the site before it became a church. Pilar has a superb view from its hilltop location to the sea.

North of Pilar is the Church of St Anne, known locally as Santana, at Talaulim. This 17th-century church has suffered neglect for many years, but the Baroque façade is still impressive and is regarded as one of the finest examples of Indian Baroque in Goa. The church hosts a feast in July, which is attended by both Christians and Hindus.

Old Goa and Divar

Known throughout the Roman Catholic world for its association with St Francis Xavier, Old Goa boasts some of India's most magnificent churches. It was a flourishing town long before the arrival of the Portuguese. Yusuf Adil, the Sultan of Bijapur, made it his second capital and a centre of trade and shipbuilding activities. After the Portuguese conquered it in 1510, Old Goa increased in size and gained importance as the capital of Goa.

Clear instructions are given at the head of the queue to see the body of St Francis Xavier

By 1684, because of epidemics of cholera, malaria and other tropical diseases, the Portuguese began to consider alternative places to site their capital. These epidemics caused the fortunes of Old Goa to decline, and eventually it was almost completely abandoned. Many of the great buildings crumbled or were stripped of their building materials, and only a few churches stand as testimony to the days when Old Goa was compared to Lisbon as a Portuguese city, to Rome for grandeur and to Amsterdam as a market. Today, Old Goa is a World Heritage Site with superbly restored and maintained churches, some of which are still in use. It is also an important Christian pilgrimage on account of its association with St Francis.

Basilica of Bom Jesus

This church is renowned for the tomb of St Francis Xavier, follower of St Ignatius Loyola who founded the Jesuit Order. Construction was completed in 1605 and the Renaissance façade shows Doric, Ionic and Corinthian design elements.

Prominently displayed on the façade is the Jesuit emblem with the letters IHS, an abbreviation for Jesus, inscribed on a tablet. Inside, the altar and reredos are lavishly gilded with a prominent image of Ignatius Loyola towering over the infant Jesus.

The main attraction for most visitors, however, is the tomb of St Francis Xavier, carved by the Florentine sculptor Fogini and gifted to the Basilica by the Grand Duke of Tuscany. His remains are in a silver casket housed in the three-tiered tomb made of marble and jasper with bronze plaques depicting scenes from his life.
Open: 9.30am–12.30pm & 3–6.30pm.
Closed: Fri and during services,
shorter hours on Sun. Free admission.

Se Cathedral

The largest church in Old Goa and one of the largest in Asia, Se Cathedral is dedicated to St Catherine, on whose day in 1510 Old Goa was captured by Albuquerque. King Dom Sebastiao commissioned the building of the cathedral in 1562, on the site of the older

church commissioned by Albuquerque, and it took 90 years to complete. Built in Tuscan and Corinthian style, Se Cathedral has a large central nave, with four attractive chapels along the aisles, and a double-vaulted ceiling. The main altar is beautifully decorated and the gilded reredos towering over it has panels depicting scenes from the life of St Catherine, including her interaction with Roman emperor Maxim, who wanted to marry her, and her martyrdom.
Open: 9.30am–12.30pm & 3–6.30pm. Closed: Fri and during services, shorter hours on Sunday. Free admission.

Divar Island
Connected by ferry to Old Goa, Divar's main attraction is the Church of Our Lady of Compassion – a rebuilt version of the older Lady Divar Church which dated from 1699–1724 – ascribed to Fr Antonio Joao de Frias, an architect and writer.

The church has an impressive Baroque façade, and its interior is decorated with attractive stuccowork, Baroque plaster decorations and altars. *Approached by ferry from the Old Goa jetty near Viceroy's Arch, Naroa and Ribander.*

Se Cathedral is the largest church in Old Goa, and is beautifully constructed in a fusion of Tuscan and Corinthian styles

Walk:
Churches in Old Goa

The best way to see the monuments of Old Goa is by
following this walking route.

*Start at the Arch of the Viceroys near the ferry for Divar and
walk to St Catejan Church, on the left-hand side of the road.
Allow 4–5 hours, including walking time and sightseeing.*

1 St Catejan Church
Built in 1661 by the friars of the
Theatine Order, which was founded by
St Catejan, this church is modelled on St
Peter's Church in Rome. The façade has
imposing Corinthian columns, niches
with statues of the Apostles flanking the
doors, and one of the few church domes
in Goa. Inside, the vaulted ceiling
displays floral patterns, while the main
altar has an elaborately decorated
reredos and equally attractive side altars.
*Walk from St Catejan Church towards the
intersection with Mahatma Gandhi's
statue. Just before the intersection, on the
right, is the side entrance to Se Cathedral.*

2 Se Cathedral
See pp32–3.
*Walk west, past the Archbishop's Palace, to
St Francis of Assisi Church in the same
complex as the cathedral.*

3 St Francis of Assisi Church
One of the most interesting churches
in Goa, this church was founded as a
chapel by the Franciscan Friars in 1527.
The present structure dates from 1661
but retains the original doorway. The
church has a beautiful interior with
heavily gilded walls and ceiling,
paintings on wood depicting the life
of St Francis, carved wood panels,
an arch decorated with floral murals,
an exquisite carved pulpit and a
dominating reredos.

The convent at the back of St Francis
Church is now a museum with sculpture
from various Hindu sites, many dating
to the 12th and 13th centuries and
showing Chalukya and Vijayanagara
styles, hero stones, *sati* memorial stones
(*sati* is the traditional Hindu practice of
a widow immolating herself on her
husband's funeral pyre) and Portuguese
bronze sculpture among the key gallery
exhibits.
*Museum open: daily 10am–12.30pm,
3–6.30pm. Small admission charge.*
*Cross the road from the gate of the Se
Cathedral complex to the Basilica of
Bom Jesus.*

4 Basilica of Bom Jesus
See pp32–3.
*Exit the Basilica on the taxi stand side
and ascend the 'holy hill' of Santa
Monica.*

5 Convent of Santa Monica

Built in 1606, and subsequently rebuilt after a fire in 1636, this was the first nunnery in India. It was abandoned in 1885 when the last sister died, and it is now used as a theological centre and a college for nuns. A part of the building houses the Museum of Christian Art, with more than 150 exhibits collected from churches and Christian homes.

Museum open: daily 10am–12.30pm, 3–5pm. Nominal admission charge.
On the other side of the road is the Monastery of St John of God, which opened in the 18th century and is now a home for senior citizens. Follow the road from the monastery to the tower of the Church of St Augustine.

6 Tower of the Church of St Augustine

A tall tower is all that is left of this church, built in 1602 by Augustinian friars. The church was abandoned in 1835 because of the Portuguese repressive attitude to the Orders.

From the tower retrace your steps to the Basilica on the main road for transport back to Panaji.

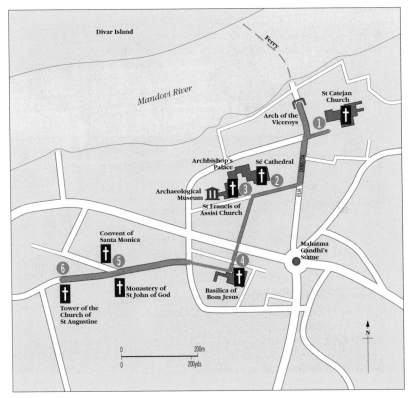

Divar Island

Ferry

Mandovi River

St Catejan Church ❶

Arch of the Viceroys

Archbishop's Palace

Sé Cathedral ❷

❸

Archaeological Museum

St Francis of Assisi Church

RUA DIREITA

Convent of Santa Monica ❺

Mahatma Gandhi's Statue

❻

❹

Monastery of St John of God

Basilica of Bom Jesus

Tower of the Church of St Augustine

200m

200yds

N

St Francis Xavier

For Roman Catholics, St Francis Xavier's association with Goa and his remains are the principal treasures of the state. He was born in April 1506 into a wealthy and noble family in Navarre, which is now part of Spain. After studying theology and philosophy in Paris, he was recruited by Ignatius Loyola into the Society of Jesus.

St Francis Xavier was sent to Goa to work in the diocese that comprised a vast area east of the Cape of Good Hope. He arrived as a 35-year-old in 1542, and remained here for a brief spell as a teacher, before moving further south. He left a deep imprint on religious life in Goa and Kerala, founding many churches and converting thousands of people.

Xavier's missions took him to Southeast Asia. On his journey back to India, he stopped at Sancian, off the China coast, and died on the island in December 1552. When he was buried, a companion put lime into his coffin. When his body was eventually exhumed and carried to Malacca it was still fresh and had been unaffected by the lime,

which normally hastens decomposition. Reburied in Malacca, the body was taken to Goa in 1554, where its incorruptible condition was considered a miracle. On examination, it was found that the body had not been embalmed and the internal organs remained intact. The mortal remains have been venerated by Catholics ever since.

First housed in St Paul's College, St Francis Xavier's remains were moved to Bom Jesus Church in Old Goa. He was beatified in 1619 and declared a Saint in 1622, by which time the right arm, shoulder blades and internal organs had been divided among Jesuits elsewhere. In 1635 the body was moved to its chapel where it is still entombed today.

Opposite: Worshippers gather at the statue of St Francis Xavier, the Jesuit missionary who ministered in Goa
Above: The mummified body of the Saint attracts pilgrims from all over the world

EXPOSITIONS

After his canonisation, St Francis Xavier's body was exposed for viewing on each anniversary of his death, but this ceased after damage was caused to his body in the early 1700s. However, official expositions resumed in order to dispel rumours that the Jesuits had taken the body when they were expelled from Goa in the 1750s. Since 1859, the body has been on view every 10 or 12 years on the anniversary of his death or on various special occasions. Since 1953 pilgrims have not been allowed to touch the remains and can only view it in a crystal container. The last exposition was from November 1994 to January 1995, when an estimated two million pilgrims visited Old Goa, and the next is scheduled for 2004–2005.

Ponda

Ponda escaped Portuguese invasion until the 18th century. It became a refuge for Hindus from the areas of the Portuguese Old Conquests during the Inquisition and temples were built to house idols rescued from destruction by the Portuguese. By the time Ponda came under Portuguese rule the Inquisition had ended and the temples were allowed to stand.

This attractive mosque is the legacy of Adil Shah

Safa Shahouri Mosque

Goa's largest and oldest mosque, Safa Shahouri, was built by Ali Adil Shah and was said to rival those of Bijapur, but the buildings were damaged when the Portuguese conquered Ponda, and subsequently fell into neglect. What remains is, however, an unusual and interesting building, with the prayer room standing on a high plinth. The mosque has a pointed pitched roof in the local style and cusped Bijapuri arches, some of which frame the windows, whilst others are purely decorative. On the south side is a tank which is used for cleansing.
On the National Highway to the west of Ponda town.

Savoi Verem

The Ananta Temple at Savoi Verem is dedicated to Lord Vishnu as *Sheshashahi Ananta*, the god who sits on the coils of a serpent. The temple has a reclining Vishnu in black stone, with a distinctive conical headdress, shown before the dawn of creation with a lotus bearing Lord Brahma, the creation god, coming out of his naval. Otherwise fairly simple, the temple has colourful wooden columns and bases in the *mandapa* (main hall).
The temple is outside Savoi village, about 10km (6 miles) north east of Ponda.

Shantadurga Temple

This is one of Goa's largest and most visited temples, situated at Queula, southwest of the main Ponda bus stop. Built by Maratha warrior Shahu, the temple has a large tank set in the hillside, a six-storey lamp tower and a tall tower over the sanctum, while the chandelier-lit interior has polished marble floors. The main deity is a form of Durga, called Shantadurga, or the peaceful Durga, because she mediated in a very fierce battle between Vishnu and Shiva that threatened to destroy the universe. Devotees believe Brahma approached Durga, who helped settle the quarrel, bringing *shanti* (peace) back to the world. The idol of Shantadurga is flanked by Shiva and Vishnu, and the temple houses a partially gilded temple car which is used for processions. It also has an octagonal drum with a lantern, showing European Christian influences on the Hindu architecture.

At Queula, about 2km (1.25 miles) off the Ponda Road.

Shri Naguesh Temple

This principal deity of the temple is Lord Shiva as Naguesh or Nangesh, lord of serpents. A tablet dates the temple to 1413, but it underwent renovation in the 18th century. A noteworthy feature of the temple is the tank, full of carp, which is surrounded by palm trees and weathered stones. Another striking feature of the temple is the *mandapa*, which has painted woodcarvings depicting the eight guardians and illustrating tales from the Mahabharata and Ramayana epics. The lamp-tower has paintings of deities near the base and Ganesh above, while the main sanctum has Shiva with the bull, Nandi. There are other shrines to Ganesh and Vishnu, as well as subsidiary ones with *lingas* (the phallic symbols under which Shiva is worshipped in his manifestation as the reproductive power).
4km (2.5 miles) northwest of Ponda in Bandora village.

Siroda

The Kamakshi temple at Siroda is dedicated to another form of Shantadurga. The temple has Linga of Rayeisvar and the image of Lakshminarayan, which were brought here from other temples in Raia on the other side of the Zuari, which were destroyed by the Portuguese in the 16th century. The temple has an unusual pagoda-style tile-roofed tower, with serpents along the roof and four kneeling elephants at the base.
South of Ponda.

Shri Naguesh Temple is dedicated to Shiva as lord of serpents

Tour: Temple Trail from Priol to Ponda

Along the road from Ponda to Priol, a distance of about 11km, can be seen some of Goa's most famous temples. *Start at Ponda and drive 4km (2.5 miles) northwest on the NH4A to Bandora. Turn onto a winding road which dips down from the highway to the Shri Nangesh Temple. Allow 2–3 hours for sightseeing and travel.*

1 Shri Nangesh Temple
See p38.
Return to the NH4A and drive towards Farmagudi, passing an interesting Ganesh Temple which blends medieval and contemporary styles. Opposite the temple is an equestrian statue of Shivaji, the great Maratha ruler, who conquered Ponda Fort in 1675.

Hindu worship often involves a musical offering to the deities

Just north of Farmagudi is the left turn for Velinga, immediately before a small river bridge.

2 Velinga
The Lakshmi-Narsimha Temple at Velinga has an image of Narsimha, the half-man half-lion image of Lord Vishnu which was brought here from Salcette, where the Portuguese destroyed many temples. Vishnu took on this form to deal with a demon to which Brahma had granted immunity from man and beast. It is a typical 18th-century temple, except for the domed tower which has some Islamic features. Inside, the *mandapa* has carved wooden columns and the main shrine has some interesting silverwork. There is a good view of the temple from the tank outside.
Return to the highway and drive north to Mardol. To the left of the highway at Mardol is the Mahalsa Narayani Temple.

3 Mahalsa Narayani Temple

The idol of Mahalsa, the Goan form of
Mohini, female form of Vishnu, was
rescued from a destroyed temple in Verna,
Salcette, and brought to Mardol. The
inner area has carved columns and
paintings of the ten *avatars* (incarnations)
of Vishnu, and the seven-storeyed lamp
tower is lit on special occasions. An arch
leads to the tank, picturesquely located
among palms and paddy fields.
*Return to the NH4A and drive north to
Priol, turning left for Shri Mangesh
Temple on a wooded hill just off the main
highway.*

4 Mangesh Temple

The 18th-century temple to Mangesh,
an incarnation of Shiva, is one of Goa's

most popular temples. The *lingam*
(singular of lingas – *see p39*) was
brought here from Cortalim when the
Portuguese took control and started
destroying temples. Previously housed
in a smaller temple, the new premises
were built for the *lingam* in the mid-
18th century on land donated by an
influential Hindu. The tank is
supposedly the oldest part of the temple,
and the lamp tower is one of the most
famous in Goa; built in Indian Baroque
style, it is painted white and shows
interesting images. The main hall is
hung with chandeliers, while the major
shrine of Mangesh is behind a carved
silver screen and shares the hall with
shrines of Ganesh and Parvati. Nearby is
the basil enclosure called *tulsi vrindavan*.

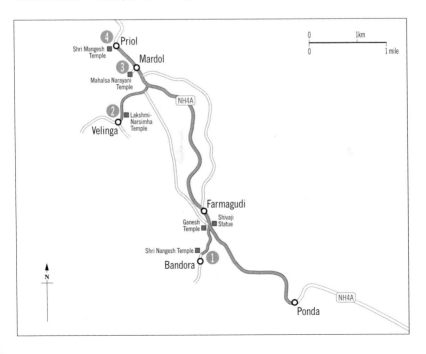

Bardez

North of the mouth of the River Mandovi, the sweeping coastline of Bardez Taluka has been a popular tourist spot for many years with its fine beaches, and enjoyable markets such as the 'Big Wednesday' flea market at Anjuna and the Friday bazaar at inland Mapusa (*see pp46–7*). Part of the Portuguese Old Conquest in Goa, Bardez has some of the best-preserved forts (*see pp44–5*) and churches in Goa.

Anjuna Beach is lined with restaurant shacks and vegetation

Beaches

Bardez has an almost continuous stretch of beach accessible from Sinquerem, Candolim, Calangute, Baga, Anjuna and Vagator. Several hundred beach restaurants and 'shacks' line the coast from Sinquerem to Vagator, with high concentrations along Calangute and Baga. With varying degrees of crowds and facilities, selecting the ideal beach is largely a matter of personal choice.

Britona

The parish church of Britona, Our Lady of the Rock of France, has an excellent location at the meeting place of the Mandovi and the Mapusa rivers. The interior is beautifully decorated with painted scenes on the simple reredos. The church has been venerated as the protector of seamen since the 16th century, when a plague epidemic threatened a fleet of ships and the captain, with his crew, vowed that they would visit the church of Our Lady of the Rock of France in Lisbon if they survived.

About 5km (3 miles) away, at Pomburpa, is an impressive church, dedicated to Our Lady Mother of God,

with Rococo decorations. The interior of the church has elaborate panelling and stuccowork tracery.

Britona is off the Panaji–Mapusa stretch of National Highway 17 on the road running to Pomburpa along the Mapusa River.

Calangute

Away from the town centre of Calangute is the Church of St Alex. The current version of the church dates from the 18th century, and it provides a good example of Rococo decoration that became a feature of Goan Christian architecture in the 1700s. Noteworthy are the false dome of the façade, the gold and white schemes of the interior, the remarkable Rococo pulpit and the fine reredos.

One of the busiest towns on the north coast of Goa, receives frequent buses from Mapusa and Panaji. The church is away from the town centre.

Colvale

Originally built in 1591, the Church of St Francis of Assisi at Colvale had to be rebuilt in 1713 after being damaged during Maratha invasions. The façade

has an impressive plaster St Francis image between two angels.
Colvale is located north of Mapusa on National Highway 17. There is a feast and fair here on 17th September.

Mapusa

Best known for its large market (*see pp46–7*), Mapusa is also the site of St Jerome Church, better known as Milagres Church. Built in 1594, it was rebuilt in the 17th century and restored after a fire in the 19th century. The church is small but attractive: inside are three retables (shelves) behind the altar which are among the most colourful in Goa. The main altar is to Our Lady of the Miracles, and there are side altars to St John and St Jerome.
Mapusa is the capital of Bardez Taluka and is an important junction for buses.

Moira

The Church of Our Lady of the Immaculate Conception dominates the village of Moira. With its flat towers and false dome, the present version of the church was built in the 19th century to replace a mud-and-thatch church, and the bell was brought here from the Jesuit College of Monte Santo. An unusual art treasure is the crucifix, which has its feet nailed separately instead of together.
Approximately 5km (3 miles) from Mapusa.

Saligao

The church of Our Lady Mother of God, built in 1873 and replacing no less than five earlier chapels, has a Gothic façade that is unique in Goa. Another unusual feature of the church is the star design on the interior ceiling.
Saligao is east of Calangute.

The palm- and shack-lined coast along Vagator Beach

Tour: Forts of North Goa

Bardez and Pernem Talukas have well-preserved forts.
Start at Panaji, turning left after Mandovi bridge and then hugging the coast to Reis Magos.
Allow about 5 hours for the tour, including travel and sightseeing time.

1 Reis Magos

The military importance of the headland of Reis Magos was recognised by Albuquerque who stationed forces here when he arrived at Goa. Don Alfonso de Noronha built the fort here in the 1550s, but it lost some of its importance in the 17th century when Fort Aguada was built.

Just below the fort walls is the colourful Reis Magos Church, dedicated to the tale of the three Magi. It was built in 1555 and restored in the 18th century, and it contains the tombs of various viceroys. The church interior is dominated by a painting on a wooden panel of the three gifts of gold, frankincense and myrrh to the infant Jesus.

From Reis Magos, travel west to Nerul, with its Shantadurga Temple, then turn left for Fort Aguada.

2 Fort Aguada

One of the strongest of Goa's forts and among the best preserved, Fort Aguada is located on a headland that offered its architects an ideal location for landward and seaward defence in 1612, after threats of Dutch invasion. It also had the advantage of natural springs providing water to last through a siege. At one point the fort had 200 cannons, two

magazines, barracks, prisons and residential quarters, and it retained its importance during the Maratha attacks of the 18th century. Today's visitors can enjoy the thick walls, the bastion on the hilltop and the old lighthouse. The road up the plateau leads to the attractive church of St Lawrence, which is a pleasant viewpoint.

From Fort Aguada, take the road through Candolim, Calangute and Baga to Anjuna. After Anjuna, a couple of roads lead to Vagator, which then runs into Chapora with its fort on a headland.

3 Chapora Fort

This fort stands on a rocky headland commanding the Chapora river estuary. Built in the 16th century by the Sultans, the fort was rebuilt by the Portuguese in the 17th century and again in 1717 to guard against threats of Maratha attacks. The fort fell to the Marathas in the same century and was taken again much later. After the Portuguese conquered the northern taluka of Pernem, the fort was no longer needed as a line of defence and was abandoned in the late 19th century. The fortifications contain Muslim tombs, ramparts and tunnels, and provide a panoramic sea view from the walls.

After Chapora comes the village of Siolim, with the Church of St Anthony and many old houses, and then the bridge across the River Chapora. After the bridge, the road cuts inland over low hills running parallel to the coast past the beaches of Mandrem and Asvem. Arambol on the way is strung out along the road, with a side road leading to the beach. After Paleim, with its Vetal Temple, the road drops down to Keri for the ferry to Terakhol.

4 Terakhol Fort

Terakhol is a tiny but strategically located fort. Built by the Bhosle dynasty of Sawantwadi in the 17th century, it is protected from the sea and has moats along the landward facing walls.

The Portuguese captured it in the 18th century and built St Anthony's Church inside, which contains a typically decorated reredos.

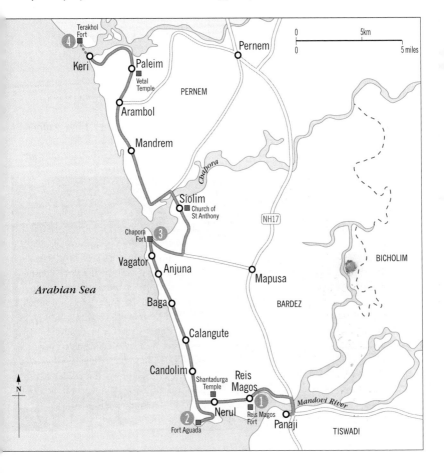

Anjuna

Anjuna's Wednesday Flea Market is famous and draws a large number of tourists. The market started as a place for long-staying western visitors, mainly hippies and backpackers, to sell belongings in order to be able to afford a longer stay at Anjuna Beach, and Indians used to come here in search of 'foreign goods' at bargain prices. From time to time, the authorities have banned the market, for instance when it became a 'black market' for imported goods and the centre of an illicit narcotics trade.

Today, the market is more organised, with 'lots' rented out for stalls where Kashmiris, Tibetans, Nepalese, Rajasthanis and Gujaratis sell handicrafts and souvenirs. The most striking vendors are the colourfully dressed Lamanis from neighbouring Karnataka who come to sell tribal jewellery and traditional textiles fashioned into anything from clothes to bags. The market is convenient for travellers who can shop for beachwear, T-shirts, swimsuits, CDs and tapes, food, second-hand books and souvenirs. There are even stalls offering services such as hairdressing, henna-painting and tattooing. While early morning is good for serious shopping before the crowds arrive, the travellers' scene builds up in the afternoon.

Mapusa Market

A market town for centuries, Mapusa is a good example of an Indian market, especially on Friday when it is very lively

Lambadi women come here to sell trinkets, mirrored bags, purses and dress material.

Margao

Margao, or Madgaon, is well known for its food market south of the municipal building. The market is a good place for fish and fruits, and the daily catch can be bought from here, including lobsters and sharks. The covered market near Old Station Road offers fruits and canned foods to clothes and household appliances. Off the tourist route, this is and colourful. Goans come here to shop for provisions such as fresh fish, vegetables, jack fruit, mangoes and plantain bananas, pickles and preserves, spices, bakery products and meats, particularly Goan sausages. There are shops and stalls selling household appliances, cooking utensils, clothes, fabrics, linen and jewellery fruits, while one lane is almost entirely dedicated to terracotta pottery. As the market has developed into a tourist attraction, Mapusa's Friday bazaar has also become a place for curios and souvenirs, and usually a good place to buy fabrics and Goan specialities which are less expensive than at the tourist markets.

Panaji

Panaji is not exactly a 'market hub' like Madgaon and Mapusa, but the municipal market is quite interesting for local colour and to see fresh fruits and the fresh catch from the fishing boats.

Opposite: Something of the old hippy spirit remains at Anjuna Flea Market
Above: Necklace vendor at Anjuna Flea Market

Bicholim and Satari

Bicholim and Satari are scenic areas of the North Goan interior, with lakes, waterfalls and the hills of the Western Ghats. They have been on the edges of political development, only becoming part of Goa after the New Conquests. Because of their remote locations, they became centres of refuge for Hindus escaping the Inquisition, and many temples mushroomed here to house idols that were in danger of destruction in the Portuguese territory.

Bus winding its way through the local countryside

Arvalem

Arvalem has Buddhist caves cut into the rocks, which have recently been converted into Shiva temples. The caves are believed to date from the 1st to the 6th centuries, and the shrines where Buddhist images stood have been converted to house *lingas* of Shiva. Near the caves are the Arvalem Waterfalls, which are most impressive during the monsoon, and nearby is the modern Rudreshwar Temple.
2km (1.25 miles) east of Sanquelim, south-east of Bicholim.

Kansarpal

The century-old Kalikadevi Temple at Kansarpal has three silver covered doors and an ornate door to the main shrine. The deity of the sanctum is Goddess Kali, and the layout is unusual in having two assembly halls leading to the main sanctuary.
At the northern end of Bicholim Taluka.

Naroa

The tiny Shri Saptokeshwar Temple is set in a beautiful forested area of Naroa (Narve). The temple is dedicated to Saptokeshwar, an incarnation of Lord Shiva, who was the principal deity of the Kadamba Dynasty when it ruled over Goa, and who came to earth pleased with the meditation of the seven sages in his honour. The multifaceted *linga*, which is the main image, was rescued from Divar Island, where the old temple

Butterfly in the Western Ghats

was destroyed to make way for a church, and reinstated at Naroa across the river from Divar during Shivaji's visit in 1668. The design of the temple is simple and it has a *Nandi* (Shiva's bull) facing the *linga*. Recently renovated, it has a lamp-tower in the tradition of all Goan temples.
Approached from Divar Island by ferry.

Sanquelim

The Datta Temple, built in 1822, lies near the bazaar of Sanquelim, a village inhabited by the Ranes of Rajasthan. The temple is situated near the foot of a palm-covered hillock, and it is visited by devotees, who believe that Dattatrai's blessings cure insanity. The interior is white marble and the main shrine displays the *trimurti* (three-headed image) of Dattatrai.

Near the family home of the Ranes is the Vithal Temple. Built in the 14th century, this Vishnu Temple has been completely renovated, but some of the wooden columns are said to be original.
Regular buses between Mapusa and Valpoi stop at Sanquelim.

Satari

The main attraction of Satari Taluka is the unusual Brahma Temple at Karmali. The Brahma image was rescued from Carambolim near Old Goa and brought to this site where it was installed in the 16th century.
Karmali Temple is 9km (5.6 miles) south of Valpoi, headquarters of Satari Taluka.

Sirigao

Sirigao's Lairaya Temple is the site for a fire-walking festival: the worshippers walk over the red-hot ashes during the festival, following ritual ceremonies performed by the temple priests.
Sirigao is northwest of Bicholim, the administrative headquarters of Bicholim Taluka.

A field sheltered by the grand hills of the Western Ghats

A joint venture of the governments of four states, Maharashtra, Goa, Karnataka and Kerala, the Konkan Railway was partly financed by revenue earned from the sale of bonds. The opening of the railway has shortened the distance between Goa and Mumbai (Bombay) by about 190km (118 miles) and created a convenient and scenic route to Kerala from Goa. The 760-km (472-mile) line is regarded as an engineering marvel as it cuts through hills and crosses bridged stretches of the coast. In all, the railway line has 92 tunnels and more than 1,900 bridges, and trains travel at 150km/h (93mph) and more.

The line crosses the entire length of Goa, and the route from Roha in Maharashtra to Mangalore in Karnataka passes through some breathtaking scenery, with views of the sea, broad rivers, paddy fields and the Western Ghats.

The Konkan Railway Corporation often works out packages for Goa that includes rail fare and resort accommodations. For more information look up www.konkanrailway.com

Chiplun

A popular midway break by road or rail between Mumbai and Goa, Chiplun is located along the River Vashishti as it flows out of Koyna River. The Parsuram Temple, about 5km (3 miles) from the town, is an important pilgrimage near the Mumbai–Goa Highway.

Ratnagiri

The heart of an important mango-producing zone and a port town, Ratnagiri is famous as the birthplace of Tilak and Gokhale, two of India's best known freedom fighters during the struggle for independence from British rule. The King of Burma was held here from 1886 to his death in 1916. Passengers also alight at Ratnagiri Station to visit Ganpatipule, a beautiful white sanded beach and an important Hindu religious centre, 45km (28 miles) away, the Jaigad Fort 55km (34 miles) from the town and the Bhagwati Temple 10km (6.2 miles) from the station.

Sawantwadi

Sawantwadi was an important nine-gun salute princely state of Maharashtra just before the Goa border. The Bhonsle rulers of Sawantwadi were constantly trying to make inroads into Goa forcing the Portuguese to build forts to protect their northern territories. Under the Bhonsle rulers, craftsmen thrived, such as the jindgars who made richly embroidered saddles, fans and furnishings, the artisans who made lacquered wood products and the makers of hand-painted playing cards called gangifa. The erstwhile ruling family has converted the darbar (hall of audiences) at their palace into a workshop for artisans to produce handicrafts, especially the gangifa cards, candlesticks, chess sets, board games and lacquered wooden furniture. The *gangifa* cards with their miniature paintings featuring religious and folk themes make unusual gifts.

Besides the historic buildings and handicrafts of Sawantwadi town, passengers also alight at Sawantwadi's out-of-town station for Amboli, a little hill station with waterfalls and views towards the sea 37km (23 miles) away, and Redi with a village, beach and Maratha Fort 20km (12.4 miles) from the station and just 3km (1.9 miles) before the northern border of Goa.

Goa

Goa's stations on the Konkan Rail are Pernem in North Goa, Karmali in Central Goa, Madgaon in South Goa and Canacona in southernmost Goa. (*See p61* for information about stops on the Konkan Railway from Goa to Kerala.)

Below: Some of the mesmerising scenery that can be viewed from the Konkan Railway

Madgaon

The capital of Salcette Taluka, Madgaon (or Margao) is the second most important town of Goa, after the state capital Panaji, and the largest in South Goa. It has a long history as a market town and as a centre of religion and learning. The town grew commercially and was given the status of a villa by a royal decree of 1778. Today, it is an important transport hub, with its major railway junction and bus services connecting Goa to other states.

Benaulim is the birthplace of Father Joseph Vaz

Church of the Holy Spirit

This typically Goan church, with a Baroque façade and ornate archway, was built in 1675 and replaced earlier versions damaged by the Muslims. In front of the church is a piazza cross that is among the most impressive in Goa and dominates the square. Inside, the church has an ornate pulpit, reredos flanked by gold pillars, and statues of St Anthony and of the Blessed Joseph Vaz (*see p53*) in glass cabinets.
Church Square, Madgaon. 6.30am–noon & 4–9.30pm.

Beachside restaurant at Benaulim

Colonial houses

Madgaon has many old houses, most of them on or near Abade Friar Road. The Da Silva House near the Church Square is locally called the *Sat Burnzam Gor* (Seven-shouldered House) and referred to as the Casa Grande. This is a large and elegant house, though only three of the seven gables that gave it its nickname survive. Still a private residence, it has a reputation for its carved rosewood furniture, chandeliers, mirrors and oyster-shell windows, but permission to visit is rarely given. Other 18th-century houses can be seen nearby.

Mount Church

Located on Mount Hill, this church offers a view over the town and the surrounding plain to the beaches.
East of Church Square.

MADGAON ENVIRONS
Beaches

Salcette has a broad stretch of beach which is home to some of Goa's best-known luxury resorts and five-star hotels. This area is usually less crowded than those on the north coast, and it is easily accessible from most of the nearby hotels and resorts. Fishing villages line the coast near the beaches, and the local towns and villages, such as Utorda, have a number of interesting old houses that can be seen from the road.

Benaulim

The Church of St John of the Good is located on a hill outside Benaulim Village. Built in 1596, it has an impressive gable façade and towers surmounted by domes. Inside, the church has a well-decorated altar and an ornate pulpit, as well as representations of the Lamb of Apocalypse from the biblical book of *Revelation*, and St Christopher carrying a child.

Benaulim is the birthplace of Father Joseph Vaz, who worked for the poor, downtrodden and Goan clergy before moving to Sri Lanka where he was known as the Apostle of Ceylon. He was baptised in the chapel of the church in 1651. *Frequent buses from Madgaon. Good stretches of beach are accessible from Benaulim village.*

Colva

En route from Madgaon to Colva, the Church of Our Lady of Mercy dates from 1630 but was almost entirely rebuilt in the 18th century. On one wall is a special altar with a small figure of Menino Jesus, who has a unique place in the history of the church. The original Menino Jesus image was brought here by a Jesuit father from Mozambique and became an object of reverence. It was moved to Rachol Seminary (*see p55*) and a new image was installed here in 1836. The Fama of Menino Jesus is celebrated at the church in October. *6km (3.8 miles) from Madgaon. Frequent buses from Madgaon stop near the popular Colva beachfront and in the village.*

A Kashmiri trader seeks out potential buyers along Colva beach

Salcette

Salcette is one of the most fertile *talukas* of Goa, producing coconut rice, cashews, fruits and vegetables. Away from its capital town, Madgaon (*see p52*), and situated inland from the coast, Salcette offers a glimpse of Goan village life and the chance to explore historic churches off the beaten track.

The well-appointed hall at Menezes Braganza House in Chandor

Chandor

This village has an interesting history as Chandrapur, the capital of the Kadamba Dynasty and a port on the once navigable Zuari River. Muslim and Christian rulers destroyed most of Chandor's historic past as a Hindu capital. The Sapta Matrika Temple was demolished in the 16th century and replaced by the Church of Our Lady of Bethlehem in 1645.

Today, Chandor is best known for its Portuguese mansions, especially those near the Church Square. The Menezes Braganza House is one of the few Goan mansions which allows visitors to view its interior: this was the home of Luis de Menezes Braganza, a journalist and

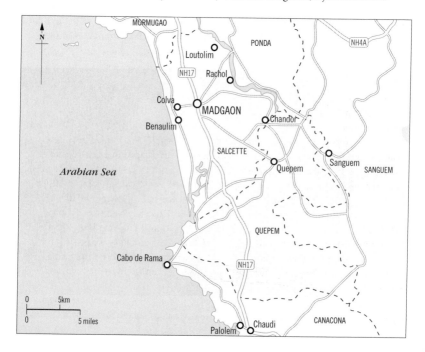

politician who campaigned for Goa's independence and for the benefit of the downtrodden from 1878 to 1938. The house was built in the 16th century but was extended in the 18th and 19th centuries. It still contains carved rosewood furniture, porcelain tiles from Macau (dating from when Macau was a Portuguese enclave in China), Italian marble and mosaic floors.

The west wing has a restored teak ceiling over the library gallery, china and porcelain which display the family crest, and a ballroom with gilt mirrors, chandeliers and gold-leaf work on the doors. The east wing has furniture with the family initials, an Italian marble-topped table and a jumble of family relics. The main treasure in the family chapel is one of St Francis Xavier's nails.

About 13km (8 miles) from Madgaon. Admission to the Braganza house is free but a donation is expected.

Curtorim

The Church of St Alex was built in 1597, rebuilt in the 17th century and renovated in the 18th century. The interior is ornately decorated and has five altars, and the towers provide a good example of the Hindu influence on Goan church architecture.

9km (5.5 miles) from Madgaon.

Loutolim

Loutolim has many old Goan houses, including the Maendra Alwares family house which is open for public viewing. Alwares also developed the complex known as 'Ancestral Goa', which offers an insight into traditional Goa, and which

has a number of recreated houses, ranging from a landowner's bungalow to a fisherman's shack and a farmer's home.

10km (6.2 miles) northeast of Madgaon. The 'Ancestral Goa' exhibition is open 9am–6pm. Separate admission charge for the exhibition and for the owner's ancestral house.

Rachol

A gateway and some walls are all that are left of the fort of Rachol, one of the most important early forts of Goa, which was built by the Muslims and captured in the 16th century by the Vijayanagara dynasty. After repairs in 1745 by the Marquis, the fort was neglected and fell into decay.

The protection offered by the fort saw the establishment of one of Goa's most important seminaries at Rachol in 1580. Earlier called the College of All Saints, it was dedicated to Ignatius Loyola in 1622. The seminary suffered when the Portuguese repressed religious Orders, first in 1759 when the Jesuits were expelled and then in 1835 when the Oratorians who replaced them also lost favour, but it once more grew into a prestigious educational centre, and today it is a forward-looking institution with a college, hospital, school and an almost self-sufficient community.

Rachol also has a church dating from 1609 and renovated in 1622 with richly gilded interiors. The altar to St Constantine houses his relics and a statue of Menino Jesus, brought here from Colva.

7km (4.4 miles) from Madgaon. Frequent buses from Madgaon stop near the church.

The South Coast

The south coast of Goa, comprising the talukas of Quepem and Canacona, has both the hills of the Western Ghats and the coastline in close proximity to one another. Plateaux and wooded valleys lie along the coast, while forests such as the Cotigao Sanctuary are just 15km (9 miles) inland.

The bastions of Cabo de Rama Fort

Beaches

Palolem is a beautiful beach, fringed by palms and known for its dolphin sightings. Its restaurants and shacks all enjoy a view of the coast, and the rocky outcrops on both sides of the curving stretch of sand are referred to locally as Pandawa's drums and footprints.

Agonda, to the north of Palolem, is a casuarina-lined beach that is growing in popularity.

Cabo de Rama Fort

This fort is named after Rama, hero of the Ramayana epic, who is said to have lived on this cape with his wife, Sita, and brother, Laxman. The fort existed on the headland for centuries, before the Portuguese conquered it in 1763 from the Raja of Sonda. It was practically rebuilt by the Portuguese but saw little action, except during the British occupation of Goa, and quietly fell into neglect.

The palm-fringed beach at Palolem is populated by boats

The spectacular coast near Cabo de Rama

Several cannons line the well-preserved ramparts, which offer superb views from the bastions. The church inside is still in use.
Buses from Madgaon.

Canacona
Canacona lies on National Highway 17, en route from Panaji to Karnataka. The St Tereza of Jesus Church was built in 1962 and lies south of Canacona town, while Shri Malikrjuna Temple, northeast of town, is said to date from the 16th century and was renovated in 1778. It has a *mandapa* with carved wooden columns. In February, the festivals of Rajasaptami and Shigmo attract large crowds.

Buses from Madgaon. Canacona is also a railway junction.

Partagali
Partagali is home to an important religious institution, Shri Sanstan Gokarn Jeevotam Math, established in Madgaon in 1475 and moved to Bhatkal in Karnataka during the Inquisition, before being established here. The huge banyan tree provides a place for quiet meditation, with a Shiva *linga* in front, which is believed to have been a pilgrimage site for centuries. In March and April, crowds gather here for an important festival, but, whilst it is still a religious establishment, the place has also developed into a centre for culture and learning.

The Western Ghats

The Sangeum Taluka of Goa covers the forested hills that form the border areas towards Karnataka in the east. This *taluka* is home to Goa's highest peaks and is inhabited by a variety of wildlife. Away from the Old Conquest areas of the Portuguese, it displays the state's oldest surviving temples and villages, where traditional handicrafts are made.

Striking stone feature of a temple in Tambdi Surla

Dudhsagar Falls

Dudhsagar Falls are among the highest in India, with a drop of more than 600m (1,969ft), and they are at their most impressive during and soon after the monsoons. The falls – whose name means 'sea of milk' – descend in stages across boulders and down rock faces, dividing and reuniting, and forming pools on the way.

The ancient Buddhist caves at Rivona are a series of monastic complexes

Rivona

The small, roughly excavated caves of Rivona are believed to have been monastic complexes, giving the area its name Rishi Van (the forest of monks), which subsequently was shortened to Rivona. The finding of a Buddha statue, dating from about the 7th century, proves that this was an important Buddhist site. The caves were later taken over by Hindus who carved their deities, including Hanuman, on the walls. Today, locals call them the Pandava Caves, named after the Mahabharata heroes, the Pandavas, who were exiled and lived in caves.

The first cave is situated near a water pump, with steps leading down to a vestibule. It has a well, a pool near the entrance porch, and tanks that store natural spring water. The other main cave is on the valley floor not far from the river.

Tambdi Surla

Tucked into the forested foothills of Sangeum, the Mahadev Temple of

Tambdi Surla is the only well-preserved structure of the Kadamba dynasty in Goa. This small 12th- to 13th-century temple is constructed from black basalt stone that must have been transported from some distance away.

The temple stands on a plinth and is entered through a *sabhamandapa* (entrance hall) with doorways on three sides, leading to the *antralaya* (middle hall) and the *garbagriha* (sanctuary) on an east–west axis. A carved screen separates the *sabhamandapa* from the *antralaya*. Four monolith carvings support the ceiling, in the centre of which are finely carved reliefs, with a lotus flower. To the east of the temple is the river, which must have been an ideal spot for ritual cleansing.

Much of the exterior wall is plain, but there are some fine miniature examples of sculpture and relief carvings. The *shikara* roof above the *garbagriha* has relief carvings of Brahma, Shiva and Vishnu with their consorts, Saraswati, Uma and Kumarashakti, and there are also some excellent carved motifs near the entrance hall.

You need your own vehicle to visit the temple.

The impressive 12th century Mahadev Temple, constructed from black basalt stone

Getting Away from It All

Although Goa is known for the 'travellers scene' at beaches, it is possible to get away from the crowded coastline by relaxing at spas, joining an Ayurvedic programme, taking up courses like diving or visiting lakes and wildlife reserves inland.

The Bronze-Winged Jacana at Carambolim Lake

AYURVEDA AND SPAS

Ayurveda, a holistic form of medicine with origins in the Indian hills, is becoming increasingly popular in Goa. Besides treatments and rejuvenation therapies, the Ayurvedic centres offer relaxing massages. The government has laid down standards for cleanliness, ensures ethical practices, and provides certification for approved Ayurvedic centres.

A number of hotels and resorts have also set up Ayurvedic centres, and some, like the Park Hyatt Spa and Resort, are also offering other spa treatments. *Some of the reputed hotels with Ayurvedic centres and spa facilities are: Cidade de Goa, Leela Palace, Majorda, Nilaya Hermitage, Park Hyatt Spa & Resort, Pousada Tauma, Taj Exotica.*

BOAT TRIPS

A number of operators offer boat trips for viewing dolphins and crocodiles along the rivers, fishing, birdwatching and water sports such as water-skiing, windsurfing and parasailing. The government has imposed safety regulations, including the provision of life jackets for passengers, but it is best to see the boat before booking a trip. In the evenings, river cruises are offered from Panaji in open and semi-open launches, with stage performances of Goan music and dance.

GOA TO KERALA

Across the border from Goa, National Highway 17 to Kerala runs through the state of Karnataka, with some interesting places along the coast near the highway. Most of these sites are accessible from stops along the Konkan Railway (*see pp50–51*).

Gokarna

Gokarna is rapidly becoming popular as a beach resort for those who want to get away from the crowds of Goa. The famous Om Beach is named after its curving stretch of sand, which resembles the shape of the Hindu *Om*, while Kudle, Half moon and Paradise beaches are also gaining popularity. The town is home to traditional temples, the best known being Mahabaleshvara Temple, with a *linga* called *Mahabala* ('the strong one'). The nearby stream is used for ritual bathing, and is considered sacred for immersing ashes after cremation.

Karwar

A stop on the Konkan Railway, Karwar has a naval port and is surrounded by islands, including Anjedive where men from Vasco da Gama's ship are believed to have found a ruined temple and water tank. Franciscan missionaries visited the island in 1500 and made their first converts on Indian soil at Anjedive. The Portuguese fort, which dates from 1505, was abandoned and subsequently reoccupied in the 17th century by the British, whose tombs can still be seen here. In 1731 the Portuguese rebuilt the fort and added cannons.

Malpe

An important fishing port today, Malpe is associated with Vasco da Gama who landed at St Mary's Isle and erected a cross.

Mangalore

Sandwiched between one of the wettest stretches of the Western Ghats and the South Kanara coastline, Mangalore makes a pleasant stopover between Goa and Kerala. One of the largest ports of South India, Mangalore traded with the Middle Eastern countries in the 15th and 16th centuries. Throughout its history, Mangalore was fought over by the local Nayaka rulers and the Portuguese until the 18th century, when the Mysore Sultans made it their shipbuilding centre. Finally, the British took Mangalore from the Sultans. The St Alosius College at Mangalore has a chapel with 19th-century murals painted by the Italian-trained Jesuit priest, Moscheni. The college campus also has an interesting museum.

The Mangaladevi Temple is named after Mangala Devi, a princess, who may have given her name to Mangalore. The 11th-century Manjunath Temple is known for its bronze image of Lokeshwara and other sculptures. *Mangalore has two stations – the central station in the city and Kakinada, a newer station 6km (3.7 miles) from the city centre. There is a good choice of hotels. There is also a beach resort at Ulal, about 10km (6.2 miles) south of Mangalore towards the northern border of Kerala.*

The Konkan Railway stops at a number of interesting sites along Highway 17 to Kerala

Udupi

Udupi is an important pilgrimage site and is the birthplace of Madhva, a 12th-century saint who set up eight monasteries in the town. The Krishna Temple here is set around a large tank that devotees believe has associations with the holy River Ganges every ten years. According to a local legend, the idol of Lord Krishna turned around to give *darshan* to a devotee from a lower caste who was not allowed access to the shrine. Another important pilgrimage is to Shri Ananthasana

Temple, which is associated with Madhva. *The station is about 5km (3 miles) from the town centre.*

LAKES
Mayem Lake
This lake in Bicholim is attractively located in a pleasant valley, just before the mining areas to the east, and it is a popular spot for pedal boating, picnics and birdwatching.

Carambolim Lake
Near Old Goa, Carambolim Lake is located between the Mandovi and Zuari rivers, with paddy fields to the south and woods to the west. It is a shallow lake, with plenty of aquatic vegetation and wild rice. It attracts a multitude of resident and winter birds: purple gallinule, moorhen, white breasted-waterhen, purple heron, pond heron, egrets, pratincole, lapwings, ibis, pied and stork-billed kingfishers, spot-billed duck and many other species can be seen for most of the year, while in winter the lake is visited by ducks and other migrating waterfowl. Around the lake, birdwatchers can enjoy wagtails, bee-eaters, flameback, woodpeckers, orioles, warblers, pipits, sunbirds, munias, weavers and other birds.

WILDLIFE RESERVES
Bhagwan Mahavir Sanctuary
This sanctuary covers an area of approximately 240sq km (149sq miles) and has an impressive checklist of mammals including panther, sloth bear, sambar and barking deer. Tigers are known to venture in at night, as well as elephants from the Karnataka border. These are rarely spotted, but visitors usually sight the odd gaur (Indian bison), spotted deer, wild boar, langur and bonnet monkeys, and striped-neck mongoose. The sanctuary and its surrounding area are rich in birdlife, with some of the key species being Malabar hornbills, Nilgiri wood pigeons, blue-bearded bee-eaters, Malabar whistling and blue rock thrushes, and red spurfowl.

The sanctuary entrance is near the crossroads at Molem, where there are places to stay and eat. Molem is also the start of hikes to Dudhsagar Falls, Atoll Gad, Matkonda Hill and Tambdi Surla. *The admission fee is to be paid at the interpretation office near Molem crossroads. Four-wheel drive vehicles are usually available on hire near the entrance for a wildlife-viewing drive.*

Pedal boating is a popular pursuit on Mayem Lake

Bondla Sanctuary

The focal point of this tiny sanctuary is its zoological park. Although the sanctuary has a long checklist of mammals, there are few chances of spotting any, except for monkeys, the odd deer and the Malabar giant squirrel, because of the visitor traffic heading to the zoo. Bondla is, however, good for birdwatching, with hornbills, crested serpent eagles, black eagles, cuckoos and woodpeckers among the many species to be spotted over a couple of days in the sanctuary.

9.30am–5.30pm. Closed: Thur. Admission, still camera, video and parking charges to be paid at the entrance.

Cotigao Sanctuary

This 105-sq km (65-sq mile) sanctuary comprises moist, deciduous forests with hills to the south and east and the River Talpona flowing through the reserve. Panther, sloth bear and other mammals live here, but they are hard to spot. This is a good area for nature treks and especially for birdwatching, with a number of species being easier to spot here than anywhere else in Goa. The villagers of Kunbis and Velpis herd livestock on the forested hillsides.

7.30am–5.30pm. Admission, still camera, video and vehicle entry charges to be paid at the entrance.

Dandeli National Park

This wildlife reserve in Karnataka lies near the Goan border. The national park is known for its good birdwatching areas, and it is also an important habitat for elephant, tiger, panther and gaur, although sightings of these are rare. The rivers flowing through the park have rapids and falls that are now used for white-water rafting.

Dandeli is 140km (87 miles) from Goa's Dabolim Airport.

Salim Ali Bird Sanctuary

This sanctuary forms part of Chorao Island, which is a prime birding area. The banks of the island along the River Mandovi offer opportunities to see storks, herons, ducks and wading birds, while the mangrove marshes of Chorao also harbour crabs and mudskipper fish.

The sanctuary is part of Chorao Island. Take the ferry from Ribander between Panaji and Ponda.

Bhagwan Mahavir Sanctuary is home to many indigenous mammals

Kerala: Land and people

According to local legend, Kerala was created by Parsurama, an incarnation of Lord Vishnu who killed more than one generation of exploitative Kshatriya clans over a period of 21 years. When he repented, the gods promised him as much land as Parsurama could reclaim with a hurl of an axe. Thus was born the entire coastline from Goa to Kerala.

A fisherman prepares his nets on Kovalam Beach

Geography

This creation myth may have its origins in geographical reality, for the coastal areas of Kerala were raised from the sea by geological forces, and the landscape has continued to evolve ever since. The rivers gushing down from the Western Ghats deposited silt along the coast, the tides of the Indian Ocean and the Arabian Sea left behind mud and debris, and eventually the land we know today as Kerala emerged. The interaction between the rivers and the tides has changed the coastline even in recent times, silting ancient ports and creating the natural harbour of Cochin that is now one of India's largest ports.

Along the coastline is the network of backwaters, a special attraction of Kerala. The backwaters have been connected to each other with man-made canals to create navigable waterways for trade, and they are now used by travellers to explore the fertile banks, plantations and villages.

Immediately inland from the coast are the rolling hills that provided building materials for the people of Kerala in prehistoric times, and which are now covered with plantations of spices and rubber. East of the hills are the Western Ghats, rising to Anaimudi Peak, at 2,652m (8,840ft) the highest summit in southern India. The continuity of the Western Ghats range is interrupted by passes, among them the Palghat Gap which gave invaders from Tamil Nadu and Karnataka access to Kerala.

The seaward slopes of the Western Ghats are richly vegetated with teak, rosewood, ebony, mahogany, silk cotton and fig trees, and most of the 5,000 plant species of southwest India can be found here, including many different types of orchids, ferns, lichen, fungi and moss. Evergreen, semi-evergreen and deciduous forests cover about 25 per cent of the state, which has some of the most substantial rainforests in India.

As many as 44 rivers cut across the Western Ghats landscape, most of them flowing west to meet the Arabian Sea, and just three heading towards larger rivers in the east. The longest rivers are Bharathapuzha, Periyar, Pamba and Beypore, and the landscape is dotted with dams and lakes that enhance the scenic beauty of Kerala.

Economy

Kerala has one of India's highest literacy rates, an excellent record for healthcare services and significant achievements in space and other scientific research. Largely unindustrialised, Kerala's economy relies heavily on remittances from Malayalis (as the people of Kerala are called) working outside the state, especially in Middle Eastern countries, and tourist revenue is becoming increasingly important. The bedrock of the local economy is agriculture, with Kerala leading India in the production of rubber, spices, lemongrass, coconuts and tapioca. Tea and coffee plantations thrive in the hills, while along the coast fishing is another important source of revenue; Kerala exports a considerable quantity of seafood.

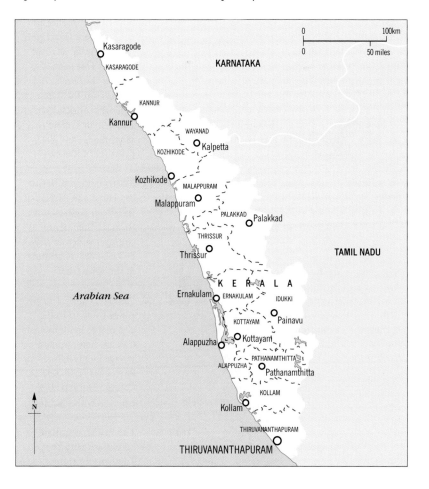

H i s t o r y

10th–5th century BC	Megalithic sites show that a sophisticated civilisation has existed in Kerala for centuries.
3rd century BC	Mauryan emperor Ashoka's edicts mention Kerala.
1st century AD	Thomas the Apostle is believed to have visited Kerala in AD 52 and introduced Christianity. Jews land at Muzuris in about AD 70.
2nd–6th century	The Cheras rule Kerala and adjoining areas of Tamil Nadu.
6th and 7th centuries	Chera power fluctuates and weakens. Malik Ibn Dinar, a disciple of Muhammad, brings Islam to Kerala, and establishes one of the first mosques in India in the 7th century.
9th century	A new Chera dynasty emerges, probably a resurgence of the earlier Cheras. *Perumal*, or ruler, was the sovereign power, but people's rights were acknowledged by the presence of elected representatives in decision-making positions. The Cheras patronise Tamil and Sanskrit literature, and gradually Malayalam emerges as a distinct language.
10th and 11th centuries	The Chola rulers of the neighbouring Tamil Coromandel coast, launch a series of offensives, bringing an end to Chera sovereignty over the Malabar coast in 1102. This paves the way for the Venads of Travancore, the Rajas of Cochin (Kochi), the Zamorin of Calicut (Kozhikode) and the Kolathiri of Kannur.
13th–15th century	Marco Polo, Ibn Battur, Ma Huan and Abdu-r-Razak, an ambassador from the Samarkand court, visit Kerala and describe the magnitude of the spice trade.
1498–1502	Vasco da Gama discovers a new route to India and makes landfall near Calicut, followed by a voyage by his fellow Portuguese compatriot, Cabraal and establish contacts with Cochin.
1625	The British negotiate agreement with the Zamorin for trade.

1653	Syrian Christians revolt against the Portuguese attempts to Latinise the church and take the 'Koonan Cross Oath' on 1st January 1653, considered a turning point in the Syrian Christian history.	**1812**	Forces are called in to crush the revolt of Kurichiyas, Kurumbas and other tribal groups of Wayanad against the policy of collecting taxes in cash instead of in kind.
1663	The Dutch succeed in displacing the Portuguese from Cochin, Cranganore, Kollam, Allepey and Cannonore.	**1836–56**	Tensions between the Hindu landlords and Muslim tenants result in many Hindu and British deaths before the revolt, called the Mapilla Riots, is subdued.
18th century	The Sultans of Mysore, Hyder Ali and his son Tipu, take northern Kerala but lose the territories in 1792 to the British, who also seized the Dutch fort at Cochin in 1795.	**1885**	The Indian National Congress is formed and instigates talks with the British.
1800	The British subjugate Kerala and divide it into the British province of Malabar, the princely state of Cochin comprising central Kerala, and the princely state of Travancore encompassing southern Kerala.	**1900**	The Tenants Improvement Act is introduced.
		1919	Kerala committee of the National Congress is convened at Trichur.
		1947	India gains independence and Kerala becomes part of Madras State.
1805	After a five-year struggle against the British, Pazzhazi Raja dies in battle and is given a hero's funeral by the British officer TH Baber.	**1956**	Kerala is given statehood.
		1957–2004	*See pp68–9 for recent political developments in Kerala.*

Governance

In 1956, the Government of India formed the state of Kerala, combining the Malabar Province, the Princely State of Cochin, most of the area of the Princely State of Travancore and Malayam-speaking areas of South Kanara District. Kerala has 20 seats in the *Lok Sabha*, the national legislative assembly (*see pp10–11*). The state went to poll for the first time in 1957, and since then, politics in Kerala have been competitive.

The Gandhi Memorial, Kozhikode

Like other states, Kerala has a governor appointed for a five-year tenure by the president of India, and an elected Council of Ministers headed by the chief minister. The State Legislature has 141 seats, with 12 reserved for Scheduled Castes and Tribes.

The people of Kerala are politically aware, active and vocal. In the 19th century, princes of Cochin and Travancore had to recognise people's appeal for more democratic practices with a legislative council and greater political access for communal groups. After the formation of the National Congress (*see pp66–7*) political activity developed and was reorganised in Kerala. The British organised an election system in their province, Malabar, in 1939.

Since independence, the people of Kerala have continued to be involved in political activities, and the turnouts for elections are generally higher than in most other states. Protest banners and street marches are common, and campaigning is lively. Trade unions and social groups participate in the political process, and the churches, too, lend their support to political parties.

Politics

In the first elections of March 1957, the people of Kerala democratically elected 'The Communist Party of India' as the single largest party in the state assembly. After mid-term polls, a three party alliance, comprising the Congress, the Praja Socialist Party and the Muslim League, came to power.

After 1964, President's rule was often imposed on the state, following no-confidence motions and inconclusive elections, until the 1980s when the Left Democratic Front and the United Democratic Front emerged as the major parties competing for power.

In the 1996 elections, the communist-led Left Democratic Front won majority in the state legislative assembly from the Congress-led United Democratic Front, but the Congress won 11 of the 20 *Lok Sabha* Seats in 1998. In the 2001 assembly elections, the United Democratic Front returned to power, reducing the Left Democratic Front to one of its lowest positions, with Congress leader AK Antony becoming the chief minister.

Political party workers are keen to play their part in the election process

Culture

Despite its unusual history of global maritime contact and European colonisation, Kerala has retained its distinctive cultural identity. For many visitors to Kerala, its tolerant culture, embracing Hinduism, Judaism, Christianity and Islam, is a particular attraction, and this is reflected in the state's dance and drama, as well as in the martial arts and alternative medicine.

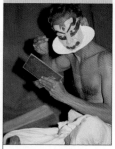

A face-painting session prior to a Kathakali performance

The caste system

The creation myth (*see pp64–5*) accords special place to Kerala's Brahmin groups, such as the Namboodris, in the social hierarchy of Kerala. According to the myth, Parsurama invited the Namboodris to settle in the new land he created with the hurl of an axe. Besides the Kerala Brahmins, Kerala also has a sizeable population of Tamil Brahmins and Sarawaswat Brahmins, the latter mainly in North Kerala near the South Kanara District of Karnataka.

The Nairs have been a dominant force in the political and social life of Kerala for a long time. They followed a matrilineal system of inheritance that many believe has its origins in the 10th and 11th centuries when Nair warriors went to battle against the Cholas. Women controlled wealth and property when the men were at war or when they died in battle. The matrilineal system could also have its origins in polyandry and polygamy, which were common practices in medieval Kerala when Namboodris had relations with Nair women. These practices became illegal in 1956 when the Hindu Succession Act gave equal rights of inheritance to men and women.

Traditionally, Nairs lived in community homes called *Tharawads*, which were designed to house the extended family. Women lived with their brothers and sisters, and their children, with shared kitchens and dining areas. Between 50 and 80 people often shared a large courtyard house called a *Nallakettu*.

Fishing is a traditional way of life in Kerala

Usually landowners, Nairs are credited with the preservation of the Kallaripayattu martial arts and the Kathakali dance drama. The Nairs continue to influence politics and have formed the Nair Service Society to promote their aims and aspirations.

The Ezhavas (tappers of toddy – the sap from the coconut palm), Mukkavans (fishing people) and Kamalans (artisans) have also formed groups to further their aims. The Sri Narayan Dharma Paripalana Yogam is working for the Ezhavas, who were previously a low-caste community, supporting political parties that promote their aspirations. With such good literacy and political awareness, there has been an enormous impact on the caste system in Kerala, especially concerning untouchability, and the domination of the upper castes has declined.

Tribes

With the state's high literacy rate, many of Kerala's tribes have seen improved standards of living, but some tribal villages still subsist on marginal agriculture and on gathering forest produce such as honey, and they have retained their traditional lifestyles. The main tribal groups – travellers of the Malayarayan, Mannan, Muthuvan, Oorali, Paliyan, Hill Pulayan, Malapandaram, Ulladan, Malayan, Paniya and Adiya – are likely to meet near tourist destinations, especially around the wildlife reserves of Idukki and Wayanad Districts. Idukki has a tribal king, Thevan Raja Mannan, at Kovilmala north of Periyar Tiger Reserve.

Language

The principal language of the people of Kerala is Malayalam, with Tamil spoken along the borders of Tamil Nadu, and Kanara in the northern districts of Kerala bordering Karnataka. English is widely spoken in the cities and large towns.

The major tribal groups of Kerala gather at such sites as Idukki, where a tribal king lives

Music and dance

See pp112–13.

Religion

Like Goa, Kerala has a Hindu majority. The Bhakti movement, propagated in the 8th century by leaders such as Sankaracharya, became popular in Kerala and resulted in a resurgence of Hinduism. About a quarter of the population follows Christianity and Kerala has a sizeable Muslim population as well.

The sacred scrolls of the Torah (teaching) in the synagogue in Jew Town, Cochin

Hinduism
See pp14–15.

Christianity
It is widely believed by the Christians of Kerala that one of Christ's Apostles, St Thomas, settled in Malabar in AD 52 and introduced Christianity in Kerala. In AD 345, a Christian Syrian Merchant named Thomas landed on the Kerala coast and preached Christianity based on the practices of the Syrian Church. In the 9th century a number of Christians from Syria settled in Kerala,

and this led to the Christians of Kerala calling themselves Syrian Christians.

The Portuguese promoted Roman Catholic practices, but the Syrian Christians resented the Latinisation of their church and took the Oath of the Coonan Cross separating their church from Rome. In 1662, however, many of the Syrian churches reunited with Rome.

The Dutch were not very tolerant of the Portuguese Roman Catholic Churches and converted churches, like St Francis, into their own Protestant ones. The British introduced the Anglican Church, and among its members were the Syrian Jacobite Group who refused to reunite with Rome in 1662.

Islam
Islam began in Mecca around the 7th century, when the Prophet Mohammad compiled revelations from Allah, and was brought to Kerala in the same century by one of the Prophet's followers, Malik Ibn Dinar. The religion

Christian Sisters serve the local community

found a tolerant society, and the support of Hindu princes like the Zamorins of Calicut helped Islam grow in Kerala. Islamic contact grew as the Arabs gained a monopoly over trade between the Zamorin-dominated Malabar Coast and the Mediterranean. The *Quran* is the holy book of the Muslims and the supreme authority on the Islamic faith. The five pillars of Islam are the profession of faith regarding the one God and Mohammed as God's messenger, worship five times daily, almsgiving, fasting in the month of *Ramadhan*, and the pilgrimage to Mecca.

Judaism

There are a number of accounts of Jewish contacts with Kerala. Some refer back to trade with King Solomon, and escaping injustice in Assyria, fleeing slavery in Babylon or the destruction of Jerusalem. Referred to as 'Black Jews', they were later supplemented by the 'White Jews' fleeing the Inquisitions of Spain and Portugal in the 16th century, and later by Ashkenazi Jews escaping the pogroms. The Jews were influential merchants, and in the 10th and 11th centuries a Jewish merchant, Joseph Rabban, was granted royal privileges by Raja Bhaskara Varma. The Raja of Cochin gave similar grants when Jews moved to Cochin after the near-destruction of the community by the Arabs in Malabar, and Portuguese prosecution. Today, only a few Jewish families remain in Cochin after the mass migration to Israel in the 1950s.

Muslim boys learn to observe the five pillars of Islam

Festivals

Besides the many religious festivals, there are exciting secular festivals, such as the boat races on the backwaters. Tourist offices can provide details of these as well as various cultural festivals at a number of tourist destinations, including Cochin, Thiruvananthapuram, Alappuzha, Kollam and Kovalam in January.

A classical Indian dance performance

Sabarimala Festival
January–February
This is one of Kerala's most important festivals honouring Ayyappan, whom devotees believe to be born from the union of Shiva and Vishnu's female form Mohini. Dressed in black, devotees make the pilgrimage to Sabarimala with stops for ceremonies along the way. Ascending the 18 steps to the temple, they promise to bring an end to sin.

Pongal
14 January
Pongal is celebrated in Tamil Nadu and much of Kerala as a thanksgiving for a good harvest. Sweets and 'first' rice dishes are prepared, and cows are decorated, bathed, fed and paraded.

Thaipuram or Thai Pussam
January–February
This festival honours Subramaya or Kartikeyan, the God of War, at his temples in Kerala. This god has six heads denoting the five senses and the mind, and is depicted on a peacock.

Krishna Festival at Guruvayoor
February–March
This ten-day festival is celebrated with processions of elephants. The Krishna image is carried on top of an elephant during the last day's procession before it is bathed in the temple tank. Ritual bathing is a feature of the festival, as devotees want to share the water with the deity.

A typical Pongal celebration in Kerala

Mannanam Convention
February
From 1894, this convention has been held in honour of Father Chavara, who is buried here and who is considered to be a saint because of his work with the lower classes. Since then, it has grown to become one of Asia's largest Christian Conventions.

Shivratri
February–March
Maha Shivratri commemorates the night when Shiva danced the *Tandava*, dance of destruction, and is celebrated with feasting, fairs and devotional rituals. Fairs take place at Alwaye and Attappady.

Thiruvananthapuram Arat Festival
March–April
This is a ten-night festival at the Padmanabhaswamy Temple in Thiruvananthapuram, culminating in a procession which carries the idol on elephant-back to the sea for ritual bathing.

Pooram
April–May
This festival is a magnificent spectacle at Thrissur, with elephants, decorated with gold, carrying beautiful parasols, and paraded to the accompaniment of drumming and firework displays.

Onam
August–September
The most important festival in Kerala, Onam celebrates the harvest and the reign of philanthropic King Mahabali. The celebrations are spectacular at

Tea plantation workers process to a Hindi temple near Munnar

Alappuzha, where boat races take place, and at Thrissur, where you can enjoy the elephant processions.

Chandakkudham Mahotsava
October
This festival is celebrated with sword play, singing, dancing, processions, elephant parades and fireworks at Beemapalli near Thiruvananthapuram. Muslims carry incense sticks to the tomb of Bheema Beevi, a woman pilgrim who travelled to Mecca and was said to have divine powers.

Other festivals include: the Malayalam Drama Festival at Kottayam (January), the Musical Festival at Thiruvananthapuram (January and February), the Mishagandhi Dance Festival (February), the food festival at Thiruvananthapuram (April) and the Ashtamudi Craft and Art Festival at Kollam (December and January).

Impressions

Although Kerala is a small state by Indian standards, especially when compared to its immediate neighbours Tamil Nadu and Karnataka, it is much larger than Goa and prior arrangements are essential to make the most of a visit to the state. With a wide variety of places to see and things to do, it can be difficult to work out an itinerary or select a tour because of the number of choices available.

The bewitching sunset at Kovalam Beach

PLANNING YOUR ITINERARY

Below are some suggestions for the best places to visit, along with ideas for things to do and see.

Art and architecture:

Thiruvananthapuram (*see pp80–81*) for Dravidian architecture, museums and art galleries; Kottayam (*see pp96–7*) for Syrian Christian architecture (including churches with murals and old plantation houses at nearby estates); Ettumanoor and Vaikom (*see pp98–9*) on the road from Kottayam to Cochin for Keralan temple architecture and murals; Cochin (*see pp102–7*) for historic and contemporary buildings; Kozhikode (*see pp124–5*) for *Mapila* (Moplah) Muslim architecture, such as the medieval mosques of Kuttichara; and Bekal (*see pp136–7*) for one of Kerala's most impressive forts. Cochin epitomises the eclecticism of Kerala with the old buildings of Fort Kochi and Mattanchery reflecting Jewish, Portuguese, Dutch, British and Hindu influences, and the modern buildings of Ernakulam, including the works of Laurie Baker, considered good examples of contemporary architecture. Cochin has beautiful murals at the Dutch palace, as well as a number of art galleries exhibiting the works of contemporary artists.

Ayurveda: Thiruvananthapuram District has a good selection of resorts offering Ayurvedic treatments at Kovalam, Chowara, Poovar and Varkala. Alternatives are the luxurious waterside resorts of Alappuzha in Kollam and Kottayam Districts, or the hotels of Kozhikode city. For serious treatments, base yourself at Kottakal, which has one of India's most famous Ayurvedic hospitals and research centres. (*See pp88–9 for more information on Ayurveda.*)

Backwaters: The most popular stretch of Kerala's extensive backwaters network is the Kottayam, Alappuzha and Kollam triangle. Cruises between these towns offer opportunities to see various fishing techniques, village activities, agriculture and cottage industries such as those using coir (fibre from the outer husk of the coconut). The northern backwaters of Kozhikode and Kasaragod Districts are developing into scenic and less busy alternatives to the better-known southern stretches.

Beaches: Kerala has a number of good beaches along the coast, stretching between Mangalore, the last city of Karnataka before the northern border of Kerala, to Kanyakumari, the southern tip of India just across the Tamil border from Kerala. Kerala's most popular beach destination is Kovalam, with a 'travellers' scene' and wide-ranging beach facilities. Marari Beach, near Alappuzha, is quite upmarket, while the northern districts of Kannur and Kasaragode Districts have excellent beaches that are likely to see significant development in the future.

Dance and theatre: Visit Cochin for Kathakali performances, Thrissur District for possible interaction with masters and students at Kerala Kalamandalam in Cheruthuruthy and Natana Kairali in Irinjalakuda, and Kannur for ritual Teyyam dances. At most other destinations (*see pp112–13 for dance and theatre and p137 for puppetry*), performances can sometimes be arranged by prior notification, but some only occur during festivals.

Flora and fauna: Visit Wayanad District for a variety of mammals and birds; Kozhikode for estuarine birdlife at Kundalani Bird Sanctuary; Palakkad District for the rainforests of Silent Valley and Parambikulam (with Annamalai in neighbouring Tamil Nadu); Munnar for Nilgiri tahr, other mammals and birdlife at the nearby wildlife reserves; Periyar for elephants and other big game, as well as lots of birdlife and nature treks; Kumarakom for birds of the backwaters; and Neyyar Sanctuary for good views of mammals and birds.

Hiking: Periyar Tiger Reserve is a great place for guided nature walks, as well as longer trekking and camping tours; Munnar for different levels of hill treks; Kottancherry near Kasaragod for short forest walks; the hills of Wayanad District for trekking, and Thiruvananthapuram District for walks at Ponmudi and Neyyar, as well as for the trek from Boancaud to Agastya Malai.

Hill resorts: Munnar is Kerala's most popular hill resort. Other popular hill destinations are Ponmudi near Thiruvananthapuram, Periyar Tiger Reserve and Wayanad District.

Sports: Thiruvananthapuram is good for golf and other sports at the clubs and government sports complex; Kovalam and other beaches for water sports; and Munnar for golf and adventure sports.

Tribal peoples: Although many districts, including Idukki, Malappuram, Palakkad and Wayanad, have populations of 'scheduled' tribes, many tribal villages may not welcome visitors. Periyar in Idukki District has a Tribal Museum in a Mannan tribal settlement that also arranges interaction with local scheduled tribes. Most of the hotels and resorts of Wayanad District arrange visits to Urali and Paniyar tribal villages.

GETTING AROUND
Boats
Boats provide a good way of seeing the landscape along the backwaters. You can take a tourist cruise or charter a whole boat.

Buses

Buses provide an economical and convenient way to reach places off the railway network in Kerala, but they are rarely the most comfortable means of transport. The Kerala State Road Transport Corporation (KSTC) has buses connecting the cities, towns and most of the important villages, but you may have to change if visiting remote places or travelling very long distances. Signs at bus stands and on the buses themselves are sometimes in Malayalam, but you are likely to find English-speaking passengers willing to help and interpret. Bus stations at the cities and at most of the bigger bus stands have information counters. Most buses have a section of seats reserved for women.

Private buses are usually more comfortable. Some operators run air-conditioned coaches, express buses and overnight 'sleeper' coaches (with bunks), but you must be prepared for loud music.

Local buses run in cities such as Thiruvananthapuram, Cochin and Kozhikode, as well as the large towns. They are a cheap means of transport, though by no means the quickest or most comfortable option.

Cars

Hiring a car with a driver provides opportunities to travel off the beaten track and see the beautiful scenery of Kerala. The rates are calculated on the basis of hours or days, with a proportionate kilometre allowance.

Cycling

Easily hired almost everywhere in Kerala, the heavy and gearless Indian bicycles are a good way of seeing some of the quieter sides of towns, or of travelling on narrow streets, but they are not really suited to long-distance travel.

Taxis

Taxis are available at airports, railway stations and at taxi stands in the cities. Like rickshaws, they usually have meters and rate charts. Alternatively, negotiate the rate for the trip before setting off.

Trains

Trains are a reliable and usually punctual method of travel on the coastal route of Kerala, from Kasaragode in the north to Thiruvananthapuram in the south. Overnight train travel saves both hotel expenses and time, and Indrail passes are convenient if you are planning to spend a lot of time on the rail network in India.

Train travel is popular and advance reservation is essential. The ticketing is computerised and there is a tourist window for those paying foreign currency at some stations, which can save the trouble of standing in queues.

A few trains, such as the Rajdhani Express, have air-conditioned first-class carriages with coupés or four-bedded cabins. Two-tier and three-tier air-conditioned sleeper cars have curtains along the aisles, and washbasins and toilets at both ends of the coach. Second class is overcrowded and uncomfortable, with filthy toilets and no bedding.

Vendors sell bottled water, soft drinks and snacks on board and at stations, and simple meals (usually based on chicken curry, egg curry or a vegetable stew with rice and accompaniments) are served on most trains, but it's a good idea to carry an adequate supply of food and water with you.

CULTURE SHOCK
Despite a high literacy rate and quality of life by Indian standards, Kerala has a number of shocks for first-time visitors, such as crowds, poverty, dust, dirt and disease. Although most people in Kerala are used to tourists, do not be surprised if visitors from other states or residents of out-of-the-way places stare, crowd around, giggle and involve you in inane conversation out of curiosity. It is perfectly common in India to discuss personal matters, politics and religion, and you will often be asked about your family and income.

Bureaucratic hurdles, slow service, crowded roads and long queues can try your patience, as elsewhere in India.

CONDUCT
Body language
Shaking hands is becoming a common form of greeting in India, but only the most westernised Indians will shake

Guarding worshippers' shoes at a mosque in Kasaragode

hands with a woman. Folding hands as in prayer is the usual form of greeting. The right hand is used for eating, receiving and giving.

Although you will see men holding hands, it is a show of friendship and rarely denotes homosexuality in India. On the other hand, any show of affection between people of opposite sexes, even if they are married, is rare in public places.

Religious etiquette
Despite an amazing religious and cultural diversity, etiquette is similar for most religious places in Kerala. You will have to take off your shoes to visit temples, mosques and churches, while smoking and shows of affection are considered disrespectful at all religious places. You should also dress modestly and not talk loudly in temples and mosques. Touching idols at temples may be prohibited. Some Hindu temples in Kerala, especially those in the southern districts, do not allow foreigners to enter the sanctuary.

Women travellers
Outside popular tourist destinations, Indians are unaccustomed to foreigners, and they may stare or pass rude comments if they see western women in bathing clothes. Away from the beaches and swimming pools, women are expected to dress modestly and not wear bikinis, swimsuits, shorts and skimpy skirts. Most Indian women do not drink or smoke. Women should have no problem conducting business in Kerala, where they are likely to be dealing with local women in many offices.

Thiruvananthapuram

The capital of Kerala, Thiruvananthapuram's history dates from the medieval Venadu dynasty that reigned over the kingdom of Travancore from Padmanabhapuram between 1550 and 1750. In 1750, Raja Marthanda Varma dedicated his kingdom to Padmanabha, a form of Lord Vishnu, and declared himself a slave of the deity. The capital of Travancore was moved to Thiruvananthapuram, literally 'the city of the sacred serpent'.

The hills surrounding Thiruvananthapuram are densely covered with vegetation

This was a far-sighted move that ensured the support of the military and the respect of his subjects for his dynasty. Irrigation schemes were introduced and Thiruvananthapuram became an important centre for the salt trade. Raja Marthanda Varma established ties with the Dutch, and also with the British who emerged as the major power in Kerala. The British intervened in the internal affairs of Travancore, when Diwan Thampi plotted against them, and under successive Maharanis, Laxmi and Parvati, the state prospered. The chief minister of Maharani Laxmi was Colonel Munro, a British officer who established public services including healthcare and education. Substantial irrigation works were undertaken and many other significant developments took place.

The golden age of Travancore was from 1829 when Swami Tirunal, son of Maharani Laxmi, proved to be an exceptional ruler, initiating wide-ranging reforms in social matters, administration, economic systems, arts and education.

Following public petitions, Thiruvananthapuram formed a legislative council in 1888, and in the 20th century opened its temples to Hindus of all castes. It was the hub of activity during the Civil Disobedience Movement against the British. *Thiruvananthapuram is 220km (138 miles) from Cochin and 382km (239 miles) from Kozhikode, with good rail connections with Madgaon (Goa) and other parts of India.*
Thiruvananthapuram also has an international airport. The tourist office is at Park View near the museums.

Padmnabhaswamy Temple

Raja Marthanda Varma rebuilt this temple in 1733, and it is said to house an idol found from the hills around Thiruvananthapuram. Unusually for Kerala, the architecture is predominantly Dravidian, with an intricately carved seven-storeyed *gopuram* (towering gatehouse) behind a temple tank. The interior of the temple is usually open only for Hindus but foreign visitors can request permission to visit in order to see the murals, sculptures and the columns supporting the main pavilions. The central shrine has images of Vishnu, Brahma and Shiva.

If granted permission to enter the temple, visitors are required to wear white sarongs (dhotis) for men and sarees for women.

Puthe Maliga Palace

Sometimes pronounced Puthen Malika Palace and also called Kuthira Maliga Palace, this building was built in the 19th century by Maharajah Swami Tirunal. The name is derived from the frieze of wooden horses and literally means the 'palace of horses'. Made from teak and rosewood, with granite columns and marble interiors, the palace houses music halls, reading rooms, an excellent library, European mirrors and chandeliers, weapons, crystal and ivory thrones, Kathakali idols, elephant howdahs (seats laid across elephant backs) and other princely memorabilia.

Open: 8.30am–12.30pm, 3.30–5.30pm. Closed: Sun. Small admission charge.

KALARIPAYATTU

This martial art is said to have evolved during the battles between the Cheras and the Cholas in the 9th and the 12th centuries. The *kalaripayattu* martial techniques became popular in the 12th century when feudal lords of the principalities that comprised medieval Kerala were constantly at war with each other. Arenas called *kalaris* were set up to train warriors for combat (*payattu* is the Malayalam word for combat). Each village had a *kalari*, near the local temple and sacred pond, which ensured a combination of health, fitness, defence, religion and hygiene. The *kalari* itself comprised a gymnasium, a temple and educational facilities. A trainer, called the *Gurukkal*, was responsible for the martial training, education and health of each member of the kalari. Training was so effective in producing skilled warriors that the British banned the *kalari* system in 1792 and the practice of *Kalaripayattu* had almost died out by the 19th century.

Training traditionally begins at the age of eight and can continue for a decade. Students are trained in the art of using wooden weapons such as the *cheruvate* (a short stick), *kettukara* (long stick) and *ottakal* (a wooden club). *Ankatari* is the technique of duelling with metal weapons, including swords, shields, spears and daggers. The most dreaded *kalari* weapon is the *umurio* sword, and training in the use of this sword is generally given only to a potential *Gurukkal*, as it is a lethal weapon.

Oil massages, traditionally used to increase the suppleness of the body, have now developed into a branch of Ayurveda. The martial art sequences of *Kalaripayattu* are said to have been adopted into the martial arts of other countries.

At Thiruvananthapuram's CVN Kalari, the *Gurukkal* trains students in armed and unarmed combat, and children begin their training at the age of eight. Another important academy for martial arts is Balacharan Nair Kalari, outside the city centre. The Kalari welcomes visitors and can arrange demonstrations.

Walk:
Colonial Trivandrum

Thiruvananthapuram, known to the British as Trivandrum, was strongly influenced by the Raj, with Maharani Laxmi appointing a British officer as the minister. As part of its colonial legacy, Thiruvananthapuram has a park with its museums, art galleries and zoo, the cantonment area called Palayam with old administrative buildings, churches and markets.

Start at the park gate. Vehicles are not allowed inside and can be left at the paid parking in a lane nearby. On your right as you enter are the Chitra Enclave and art galleries displaying the collections of artists such as KCS Panikar, as well as temporary exhibitions. The centrepiece of the park is the Arts and Crafts Museum.

Allow about 4 hours, including sightseeing, plus some time to browse and to shop at Connemara Market.

1 Arts and Crafts Museum

Formerly called the Napier Museum, this government arts museum was founded in 1880 and was designed by Chisolm, an architect known for his eclectic architecture. The colourful façade has European, Indo-Saracenic, Keralan and Chinese Pagoda features. The museum has an excellent collection of 12th-century bronzes, 15th-century woodcarvings, temple chariots, gold jewellery, Javanese objects, Kathakali figures and a model of the Guruvayur temple. To the east is the Natural History Museum, which houses a model of a Nair *Tharawad* (wood and stucco house), explaining the different parts of a

Nalakettu, a traditional courtyard house of Kerala, complete with Kathakali dance drama and an elephant procession.
Open: 10am–5pm, Wed 1–4.45pm. Closed: Mon. Small admission charge. To the north of the Arts and Crafts Museum is the Shri Chitra Art Gallery.

2 The Shri Chitra Art Gallery

This gallery exhibits a collection of Raja Ravi Varma's portraiture, as well as a variety of works of Rajasthani, Tanjore, Balinese, Mughal, Chinese, Japanese, Tibetan Buddhist and South Indian art.
Open: 10am–5pm, Wed 1–4.45pm. Closed: Mon. Small admission charge. Next to the Shri Chitra Art Galley is the entrance to the Botanical and Zoological Park.

RAVI VARMA'S PAINTINGS

Raja Ravi Varma (1848–1906) was one of India's first artists to take up oil painting, to master perspective and to use human models for Hindu deities. He was awarded the Vira Sanghala Decoration by the state of Travancore.

3 Botanical and Zoological Park

Established in 1859, this park is worth visiting for its zoo, which is one of the largest in India. The botanical garden has many interesting trees and plants.
Open: 9am–4.45pm. Closed: Mon.
From the exit of the Zoological Park, follow the path along the side of the Arts and Crafts Museum to the main gate, then turn right and walk past the tourist office, taking the right fork after the intersection. You will see the Victoria Jubilee Hall on Mahatma Gandhi Road, and St Joseph's Cathedral on your left.

4 St Joseph's Cathedral

This 19th-century cathedral is one of the oldest churches in Thiruvananthapuram, with a tall tower and a red-brick façade expressing Gothic influences. The church has some interesting British tombstones to the rear.
Turn left at the gate and walk along Mahatma Gandhi Road. Connemara Market is on your right, just off the main road.

5 Connemara market

This old market has a granite entrance and overhanging roofs supported by brackets.
Retrace your steps to the car park next to the park entrance, or take public transport from the market entrance.

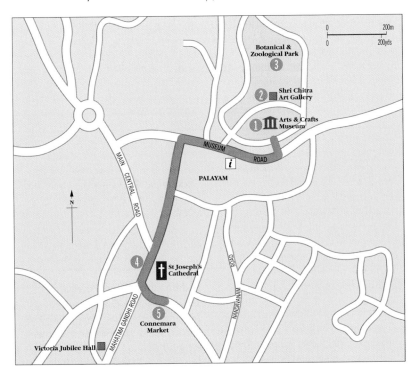

Thiruvananthapuram Environs

Situated along the coast where the Western Ghats come fairly close to the sea, Thiruvananthapuram is the starting point for trips to lesser-known beaches and minor hill stations. The excursions are good options for those who want to get away from the crowds of the state capital city and the travellers scene at nearby Kovalam (*see p86*). As the southernmost district of Kerala, Thiruvananthapuram also makes a base for trips across the Tamil Nadu border.

A swift tea-break at a roadside stall near Trivandrum

Kariavattom

North of Thiruvananthapuram, Kariavattom is home to Kerala University and the Technopark, a computing and business centre. The university library has a superb collection of palm-leaf manuscripts in numerous languages, besides copper inscriptions and paper manuscripts, initiated by the Travancore Princely State.
15km (9.3 miles) from Thiruvananthapuram. The library is usually open from 10am–4pm Mon –Fri except during the university's holidays.

Nedumangad

The renovated Koyikkal Palace Nedumangad has a folklore museum containing musical instruments and folk arts, and a fine coin collection.
About 18km (11 miles) north of Thiruvananthapuram. Open: 9am–5pm. Closed: Mon.

Neyyar Lake

About 32km (20 miles) from Thiruvananthapuram, Neyyar Lake is the focal point of the 128-sq km (80-sq mile) Neyyar Wildlife Sanctuary. Here you are likely to see elephants, tigers, bear, gaur, deer and wild boar, but be warned – they are hard to spot. The higher ranges are covered by grassland inhabited by the tahr (a goat-like mammal) and other herbivores, but trekking permits are essential. There is a lion safari park, where some lions can be seen in an enclosure, and a crocodile park.

The Sivananda Yoga Vendanta Dhanwantari Ashram overlooks Neyyar Lake and conducts yoga classes for beginners, advanced students and teachers.

The Agastya Hills, some of the highest in Southern Kerala at 1,869m (6,230ft), can be seen from the lake on a clear day.

Padmanabhapuram Palace

This seat of power of Travancore State is now officially in Tamil Nadu. The name literally refers to the lotus emerging from the navel of Lord Vishnu to whom this palace was dedicated by Raja

Marthanda Varma. The palace was the residence and administrative headquarters of the Venadu dynasty before they moved to Thiruvananthapuram in 1750, and its oldest parts probably date to the 1550s. Built from teak and supported by granite, it is an excellent example of Keralan architecture, showing the woodcarving that has been characteristic of Kerala's art, as well as some fine murals and well-sculpted stone figures.

The palace comprises the royal dwelling quarters, the administrative areas, public spaces and a shrine. The interior is exquisite, especially the entrance hallway with its carved rosewood ceilings, and the Durbar hall that has floors finished with crushed shells, egg whites, coconuts and juices, and windows adorned with coloured mica.

Open: 9am–5pm. Nominal admission charge, camera and video charges.

Ponmudi

At an altitude of over 1,000m (3,333ft), Ponmudi is a lightly wooded hill resort. Banana, rubber, spice and tea plantations can be seen on the road up from Thiruvananthapuram, and the area is well known for its pleasant walks.

Varkala

Varkala is a town with a famous Krishna Temple, Janardhana Temple, which was largely rebuilt in the 13th century. It has some very old banyan trees, and the subsidiary shrines are said to be older than the temple itself. There are Saivite shrines outside the main complex, and on the cliff near the temple is the old palace of the Travancore Princely State, which has been converted into a government guest house. Another attraction is Papanasam Beach at Varkala, which has been developed into a popular resort.

Veli Beach

Veli has been developed as a tourist park along the shores of a lagoon stretching out to sea, and ending in a sandbar and a good beach with boating facilities. The landscaped gardens of the park contain fine sculpture by Canai Kunuram, known for their balance, harmony, and erotic elements!

Spice plantations are an integral part of the local landscape

Kovalam

Kovalam was the beach resort of the Maharajas of Travancore. Western tourists discovered its charms in the 1960s and 1970s when, like Goa, it became a 'hippy hangout' and started attracting backpackers and package holidaymakers. Today, Kovalam is one of Kerala's most popular tourist destinations and it rates among India's most visited beach resorts.

The coast along Kovalam – an earthly paradise

Beaches

Kovalam's main claim to fame are its four stretches of beach, separated from one another by rocky promontories or streams. Most of the tourists visit Hawah Beach (or Eve's Beach), and Lighthouse Beach near the striking red-and-white lighthouse on the headland.

Samudra Beach, about 4km (2.5 miles) north, is becoming an increasingly popular option. Some 8km (5 miles) south of Kovalam, beaches like Chowara and Pullukudi are gaining popularity as alternatives. Chowara is home to some of Kerala's best-known Ayurvedic centres.

One of four stretches of beach that make Kovalam a much sought-after holiday destination

EXCURSIONS

Aruvipuram

Literally 'the village of flowing waters', Aruvipuram on River Neyyar attracts many pilgrims for ritual bathing, since the pilgrims believe that the river waters have healing properties. Pilgrims usually use the steps to wash their feet, but the waters are torrential so swimming is unsafe.

Kanyakumari

A visit to Kanyakumari, the southern tip of India where the Bay of Bengal and the Arabian Sea meet the Indian Ocean, undoubtedly forms the most popular day excursion from Kovalam. Kanyakumari means 'virgin maiden' and refers to Devi Karna who sought to become Shiva's consort by doing penance at the tip of India. When she was unsuccessful, Devi Karna proclaimed she would remain a virgin. The temple to Devi Karna overlooks the sea and is the site of one of the most important pilgrimages for Hindus. Devotees consider her to be the protector of the Indian shores. The Vivekanand Memorial is situated on a rock offshore from the mainland and gives spectacular views; it is dedicated to Swami Vivekanand who visited in 1892 as a devotee of the virgin goddess and stayed on to meditate. Inspired by his meditation, Swami Vivekanand spoke at the Parliament of Religions at Chicago and founded the Ramkrishna Mission at Chennai. The memorial built in 1970 integrates temple architectural styles from different parts of India.

Neyyatikara

The Shri Krishna Temple at this site dates from the 18th century and is historically significant as Raja Marthanda Varma is said to have stayed here during a conflict.

The town is 20km (12.4 miles) from Thiruvananthapuram on NH 47. There is a holy bathing site on the Neyyar River about 4km (2.5 miles) from the town.

Padmanabhapuram

See pp84–5.

Suchindram

Unusually, the temple at Suchindram is shared by the trinity of Vishnu, Brahma and Shiva. The temple has an ornately decorated towering *gopuram* (temple gatehouse), and to the north is an enormous tank with a shelter in the middle. Founded during the Pandiyan reign, which reached its zenith in the 12th and 13th centuries and expanded under the Nayakas of Thirumalai in the 17th century, the temple became part of the Travancore Princely State and houses treasures from different kingdoms. Among the interesting sculptures are those depicting Shiva, his consort Parvati, and his sons, Ganesh and Subrahmanya, as well as a towering Hanuman statue inside.

Usually open to non-Hindus. Sunset ceremonies on Friday.

Vizhinjam

This was the capital of the Ay rulers who were a dominant force in Travancore's history. Once controlled by the Pandiyans in the 7th century, the Ay rulers rose to prominence 200 years later. Now largely a fishing village, Vizhinjam has an 8th-century shrine with figures cut into the rock.

The Home of Ayurveda

Ayurveda probably started in the Himalayas in about the 6th century BC, and is a type of herbal medicine which is used in most parts of India. It is associated with Kerala on account of the many colleges and hospitals, such as the one at Kottakal, and the many Ayurvedic resorts that have recently become established in the state. The word *Ayurveda* is derived from the Sanskrit words for 'wisdom', or 'science', or 'life', and the philosophy is based on a holistic understanding of the human body, mind and spirit; illness affects both the body and the mind, and these should therefore not be treated separately. Physical and emotional health can be maintained by balancing energies, and diagnosis is based on the philosophy that illness is the result of a loss of balance of *doshas*, a combination of elements that comprise the human body, making use of the 107 *marmas* or sensitive points. Ayurvedic physicians prescribe traditional healing techniques such as purification, diet, herbal medicine, massage, meditation and yoga.

Ayurveda was discouraged by the British Raj, but following independence in 1947 the government of India promoted Ayurveda as an important form of medicine.

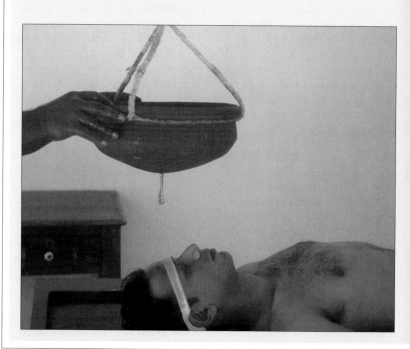

For most visitors to Kerala, the most enjoyable and relaxing Ayurvedic treatment is a massage, which is also the first cleansing therapy offered to most patients as a form of pre-detoxification. The massage oils have properties that help to heal and protect the skin; the therapist uses gentle, circular movements – with the degree of pressure depending on the patient's condition – covering the head and the body, and the massage is followed by a steam bath. Some resorts also offer synchronised massages by two or more therapists, as well as Chavatti-Uzhichil, which is done by foot instead of by hand, for rejuvenation, muscle toning, weight loss and improved circulation.

The Ayurvedic programmes offered by most hotels and resorts are *Rasayana Chikitsa* (rejuvenation therapy), *Kayakalpa Chikitsa* (body immunisation and longevity therapy), *Sveda Karma* (involving body cleansing by inducing perspiration as part of pre-detoxification) and *Panchakarma* (for overall well-being). Many resorts provide programmes for patients suffering from rheumatic and arthritic problems, backaches and chronic ailments. Meditation, yoga and stress-relief programmes are also popular.

The treatments on offer at Ayurvedic resorts include the following:

Dhara: In Sirodhara, a thin flow of herbal oil, from a pot with a hole suspended over the patient's head, is directed to a spot on the forehead near the eyebrows and then stroked down the hair by the therapist and allowed to permeate the skin. The oil may be massaged into the scalp if prescribed by the physician. Other forms of *dhara* involve the pouring of buttermilk, fermented yoghurt-based fluids or medicated milk over the forehead or body.

Karnapoornam: Ear treatment.

Marma Kizhi: Massage with herbal powder-filled cloth bags.

Nasyam or Nasya Karma: Nasal therapy, which involves inhaling medicated vapours.

Pizhichil: A herbal compress.

Sirolepam: Application of herbal pastes chosen for the patient.

Snehapanam: Administers ghee internally for patients of osteoarthritis, leukaemia and other ailments.

Sveda: Induces perspiration by application of herbal bundles, along with medicated steam baths or herbal tub baths.

Tharpanam and Ajanam: Eye treatments.

Udvarthanam: Herbal powder massage.

Urovasti: Administration of oil to the chest.

Opposite: *Dhara* – an Ayurvedic treatment involving a flow of herbal oil onto the patient's forehead

Kollam

Surrounded by coconut palm and cashew plantations, the market town of Kollam, or Quilon, is situated on the edge of Ashtamudi Lake. As one of the gateways to the waterways of Kerala, Kollam was an important trading city coveted by colonial powers, and some of its old, red-tiled wooden houses still line the narrow, winding streets.

A truck loaded with coir, which will later be woven

Known to Marco Polo as Koilum, it traded with Europe, the Middle East and China, and evidence of Chinese connections still survives in its ceramics and in the style of fishing nets lining the backwaters.

In the 9th century, Kollam was the capital of the Venadu Dynasty, and at that time Raja Udaya convened a special meeting to announce the dawn of a new era in 825. Today, Kollam is known as a convenient staging post for boat trips on the backwaters.

Kollam is 71km (44 miles) from Thiruvananthapuram, 145km (90 miles) from Cochin and 333km (208 miles) from Kozhikode, with good road and rail connections.

Ashtamudi

Literally 'seven creeks', Ashtamudi Lake extends north from Kollam. It is an attractive lake with palm-fringed banks and promontories extending into the water, where dugouts carry coir, copra (coconut kernel), cashew and fish. Boat tours on the canals of Ashtamudi provide a good way of experiencing village life, coir weaving, copra drying, fish and shrimp farming, matchstick making and agriculture.

Church of Our Lady of Velamkani

One of the landmark buildings of Kollam, this is an unusual-looking Christian shrine, in the shape of a pyramid and topped by a golden virgin. *Situated near Alappuzha Road.*

Thangaserri

Thangaserri was dominated by the 16th-century Portuguese Fort Thomas, now largely in ruins, which was later taken by the Dutch. It became an important British outpost and has some interesting old churches and a lighthouse.

KOLLAM ENVIRONS
Kayyamkulam

North of Kollam, Alamakadavu on the outskirts of Kayyamkulam is a centre for the construction of Kerala's rice boats, called *Kettuvalams*.

Krishnapuram Palace

Raja Marthanda Varma built this palace near Kayyamkulam in the 18th century, probably expanding older royal residences that existed here. Renovated in 1999, the two-storey palace is a good example of Keralan architecture, with gabled roofs and woodcarvings, and it still has its original bathing tank inside. The palace contains the mural of *Gajendra Moksha*, one of the largest wall paintings in Kerala, depicting the Bhagwad story of the deliverance of the elephant chief by Lord Vishnu.

Now a museum, the palace exhibits sculptures and paintings from various archaeological sites and copies of murals from Matancherry Palace, as well as some from other temples and churches. One of the prized exhibits is a palanquin (a covered seat enclosed by curtains and carried on men's shoulders) of the married women of royal family, and an ancient Buddha statue stands in the landscaped garden.

Open: 10am–1pm, 2–5pm. Closed: Mon. Small admission charge.

Valliakvu

Also called Amrithapuri, Valliakvu is home to the ashram of Matha Amrithanandamayi, whose Mission Trust supports a variety of projects such as orphanages and hospitals.

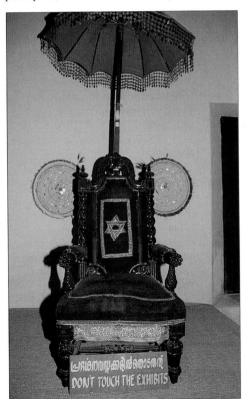

The old raja's throne, Krishnapuram Palace

KETTUVALAM

Kettuvalams are strong and sturdy boats capable of carrying heavy loads. Often called rice boats, the *Kettuvalams* are used for cargo and as a means of transport, and they are made from wooden planks tied together with coir and coconut fibre, with a thatched roof to protect people and cargo from the rain. In deep water the boatman uses an oar to propel the boat along, but in shallower water he uses a long bamboo pole, rather like the sort used in a punt.

The *Kettuvalam* declined in importance when road transport began to make most of the waterways redundant, but today many of them have been redesigned and remodelled as passenger boats and houseboats (*see pp140–3*).

Alappuzha

Alappuzha, or Allepey, is a market town clustered along a network of canals. The waterways are still in use and service the coir industry that has thrived here since the 19th century. Another important industry here is cashew processing, and some of the old factories and warehouses still stand.

Alappuzha is 71km (44 miles) from Thiruvananthapuram, 145km (91 miles) from Cochin and 333km (208 miles) from Kozhikode, with good road and rail connections.

Traversing the backwaters of Alappuzha

Temples

The Mullakal Devi Temple is among several that participate in a festival every December, which is celebrated with music, dance, rituals and processions. Alappuzha also has a modern Jain Shwemtambar temple built next to the older Jain shrine.

Jain temples are open 6–8am & 4.30–8pm.

ALAPPUZHA ENVIRONS
Ambalapuzha

Sree Krishna Ananda Temple at Ambalapuzha is one of the most important temples of the erstwhile Travancore State. Designed in typical Keralan style, with gabled roofs and carved wooden façades, it is set beside a sacred tank. Milk rice, which is offered at the temple, is considered as the gift of a Brahmin to the poor.

About 14km (8.5 miles) south of the town centre.

Aranmula

Aranmula is well known as the centre of bell-metal handicrafts, and especially for its famous mirrors. It has a Parthasarthy Temple to Lord Krishna as the charioteer to Arjuna in the Mahabharata. Arunmala is also the site for a boat race which is more a procession than a competition, with devotees believing that Krishna is in every boat.

Arthungal

The St Sebestan Church at Arthungal was built in 1591 and is well known for the procession that carries the saint's statue to the beach each January.

About 25km (15.5 miles) north of the town centre via Mararikulam.

Haripad

Haripad has one of Kerala's most important Subrahmaya Temples, which houses an idol of the four-armed deity which devotees believe was found in the river.

South of Alappuzha on NH 47 leading to Kollam. Haripad is one of the major centres for boat-races and festivals in August and December.

Mannarsala

The Nagaraja Temple at Mannarsala is one of the most important of the many temples located in the 'snake groves' of Kerala. The surrounding woodlands have several statues of snake gods and hooded cobras among the trees and along the paths leading to the temple dedicated to the Snake King, Nagaraja. Childless women visit the shrine to pray for a child, and, if they have one, they return to donate the equivalent weight of the baby in grains to the temple.

The temple is best known for its association with the Mahabharata which mentions the fleeing of snakes to a place devotees believe is Mannarsala. Unusually, the temple has a priestess as the local Namboodri Brahmin women are said to have planted sacred groves for the snakes. In typical Keralan architectural style, the temple's main shrine is dedicated to Nagaraja, the serpent king, and his consort.

Thousands of Hindus attend the temple's annual festival in September or October, when its idols are carried through the woods, and offerings of milk, rice and turmeric are made. *About 32km (20 miles) south of Alappuzha.*

Mararikulam

The fishing hamlet of Mararikulam provides access to the excellent Marari Beach, which is becoming a popular resort.

A boat ferries a family safely across the water in Alappuzha

BOAT RACES

On the second Saturday of August, the Nehru Boat race at Alappuzha is one of Kerala's most famous regattas, and thousands come to watch the race on Vembanad Lake. Behind the stern of each snake boat, shaped like the hood of a cobra, a hundred or so rowers power their way across the waters, shouting and singing enthusiastically. The rowers are supported by helmsmen and women, who do the steering, and cheered by singers and spectators from their village. The crowd avidly watches a tradition that harks back to the time when the snake boats transported troops to the battle.

Boat races are also a feature of the Onam celebrations elsewhere in Kerala. At Payipad near Haripad, the boat races are said to be in honour of the finding of the idol of Subhramanya at Haripad, whilst at Arunmala the boats carry effigies of Lord Krishna.

A unique aspect of Kerala's geography is its backwaters, a network of rivers, streams, lagoons, lakes, canals and tanks that run along most of its coastline. The best-known stretch is from Kollam to Kochi, the northern section of which is called Kuttinad. The backwaters have few outlets to the sea and the lagoons depend on rivers for their water. In the monsoon season, sea water enters parts of the inland lagoons and canals: this combination of saline and fresh water is essential to the aquatic life of the backwaters, including the coveted *karimean* fish.

Touring the backwaters is the one of the highlights of a visit to Kerala. Waterfront activities like coir-making, rice growing, toddy-tapping and fishing can be seen along the banks, and traditional dugouts ply the waterways. The banks are green with coconut palms and groves of mango, papaya, jackfruit and other trees, and tapioca is among the crops grown here. Travelling the backwaters also gives a glimpse of village life; entire settlements are located on strips of land separating the waterways, and the houses have poultry, cattle, pigs and ducks, and even vegetable gardens. Prawns and fish are farmed, sand is dredged for construction, and shells are collected for the production of lime. The boats pass canals where coconuts, coir, cashews and food are loaded onto dugouts.

The most popular backwater trip is the journey from Kollam to Alappuzha, or vice versa, which takes about eight

hours, usually departing at 10.30am, with halts along the way, to the coir village of Thrikkunnapuha, to islands such as Lekshmithuruthy, and to popular spots such as the ashram at Amrithapuri. Shorter trips are also available from Kollam, Alappuzha and Kochi, and from the northern backwaters near Calicut and Bekal. Some cruises, such as those from Alappuzha and Kottayam, include toddy tasting in their itinerary.

Apart from tours, passenger boats and public ferries, it is also possible to hire motorboats and speedboats for travelling the backwaters. Hotels and resorts at Kottayam, Kumarakom, Alappuzha and Kollam also organise backwater cruises and short boat trips. The best, but more expensive, option is to charter a houseboat.

Opposite: A boatman cruising along the backwaters
Above: Chinese fishing nets are a distinctive feature of the backwaters

TROUBLED WATERS

Although travellers see a somewhat idyllic side of life on Kerala's backwaters, these areas are not free of environmental problems. Reclaimed land for agriculture has reduced the surface-water area, and almost all the mangrove vegetation has been destroyed. The construction of barriers across Vembanad Lake is one of the many changes that have affected the ecology, along with increased population density and pollution.

Kottayam

Kottayam is sandwiched between the hills to the east and the backwaters to the west, with fertile lands on the outskirts producing rubber and other cash crops. The Christian population of Kerala followed the Syrian Orthodox Church, but following attempts by the Portuguese to Latinise the Church, the Syrian Christians took an oath stating that the Portuguese priests were not their leaders.

The highly-adorned altar of a Syrian Orthodox Church in Kottayam

The Syrian Church became an autonomous body without links to Rome. Many Syrian Christians subsequently rejoined the Roman church after a visit by the pope, but one group formed the Jacobite Syrian Christian Church. After independence, most of the churches reunited, and Kottayam's history of Syrian Christian settlement is reflected in its churches.

Kottayam is also known for its high literacy rate, and it publishes some of the most read Malayalam newspapers and magazines. Many well-known Malayalam writers hail from Kottayam, and a writers' cooperative was established here in 1945.

Cheria Palli

The elegant St Mary's Church, called Cheria Palli, is some 450 years old and is situated on top of a hill. Its interior displays some beautiful murals on the walls and ceiling, and above the altar.
North from the town centre. Sunday mass at 9am.

Thirunakkara Shiva Temple

This temple is in typical Keralan style,

with an interesting *Kootiattum*, the traditional temple theatre for religious dance drama.
In the centre of town.

Velia Palli

This church was built in the 16th century and is famous for its Persian Cross with a Pahlavi inscription next to the altar. Another cross has Syriac liturgy. There is also an unusual portrayal of St George slaying a dragon. The guest book has comments dating from 1899, and among its entries is one by an Ethiopian emperor.
North from the town centre. Sunday and Wednesday mass at 7.30am.

KOTTAYAM ENVIRONS
Chengannur

Chengannur has three interesting temples – a Mahadev Temple with a theatre on an old plinth, a Bhagwati Temple, which is said to bring good fortune to devotees, and a small 18th-century Narsimha Temple.
About 30km (18.5 miles) south of Kottayam, 1km (0.6 mile) off the highway to Thiruvananthapuram.

Ettumanoor
See pp98–9.

Kaviyur
Kaviyur has one of Kerala's best-preserved caves, dating from the 8th century and notable for its carved reliefs. It also houses a pillared hall, a shrine and a *linga*.
5km (3 miles) from Thiruvalla on the rail route to Thiruvananthapuram, east of the main road.

Kumarakom
With its bird sanctuary, backwater villages and islands, Kumarakom has seen the development of tourist resorts around it. Here you can arrange boat trips to see the birdlife, which is at its best from November to February when migrants from the north make it their winter home. This is also a good spot to experience traditional farming life and village activities.

St John's Cathedral
Designed by Laurie Baker, this Syrian Christian church is built in Keralan architectural style with a tiled roof, timber ceiling and a circular interior that has no visible support. It was built to mark the anniversary of the martyrdom of St Thomas.
On the road to Tiruvalla from Kottayam.

Tiruvalla
Tiruvalla is home to the Shri Vallabh Temple, which is noted for its night-time Kathakali performances.
South of Kottayam on the road and rail route to Thiruvananthapuram.

Syrian Orthodox Christians celebrate St George's day in Kottayam

Tour: North of Kottayam

The road north from Kottayam to Kochi criss-crosses rivers and backwaters, and two of Kerala's most important temples can be seen on this route.

Drive 12km (7.5 miles) north from Kottayam towards Kochi. The Shiva temple of Ettumanoor is on the right-hand side, with parking available on the road heading east to Palai.

1 Ettumanoor

The Mahadev Temple at Ettumanoor is one of the wealthiest in Kerala. Built in the typical Keralan style in the 16th century, the temple is noted for its woodcarvings. Beautiful murals depict Vishnu in the form of Padmnabha reclining on a serpent, and Shiva as Natraj crushing evil on the *gopuram* (gatehouse), as well as the lives of Rama and Krishna, and Shaivite figures in the halls. The murals are similar in style to those in the Mattancherry Palace of Cochin (*see pp106–7*). The main shrine is circular, with a conical, copper-clad interior ceiling and enclosing a square sanctuary. There is a large festival here in March, when gold elephant statues are put on display.

A hilly road travels east from Ettumanoor to Palai, passing rubber plantations on the way.

2 Palai

Palai, or Pala, has two important and impressive churches, one of which is believed to date from the 11th century. Palai also boasts the Shrine of Our Lady of the Immaculate Conception with a tower, as well as a number of old Syrian Christian houses on the rubber plantations.

Retrace your tracks from Palai to Ettumanoor, and then turn right on the road to Cochin, until you come to Vaikom.

Rubber tapping at a plantation

3 Vaikom

Vaikom is one of the holiest Shiva temples in Kerala and is enshrined in myth. The temple's present structure probably dates from the 16th century and its murals are probably 18th century. These depict Shiva, Parvati and Ganesha, Vishnu with his consort, and a number of other figures.

In 1925, the temple was one of the first to allow untouchables to visit the main sanctuary. By 1928, the Maharaja of Travancore opened temples to Hindus of all castes throughout his princely state.

The temple has a 12-day festival in November and December, with a particularly auspicious last night. Deities from nearby temples are brought here throughout the festival.

From Vaikom you can drive back to Kottayam or continue on the road to Kochi.

THE PILGRIMAGE TO SABARIMALA

Kottayam lies on the route of the famous pilgrimage to the Ayyapa Temple of Sabarimala from Thiruvananthapuram. After Kottayam comes Erumeli where thousands of pilgrims, dressed in black, worship at a mosque dedicated to Varr. From Erumeli, the 60-km (38-mile) track has to be covered on foot, passing Challakayam and Pampa, with stops for ceremonies at a number of pilgrim sites en route. Pilgrims have to face a steep, two-hour jungle walk to the shrine, which is 914m (3047ft) above sea level. Eighteen golden steps symbolise various sins, and when ascending the steps, pilgrims take an oath to give up these sins.

Those who do not want to make the entire pilgrimage can take a bus to Chalakayam and then walk 8km (5 miles) to Sabarimala.

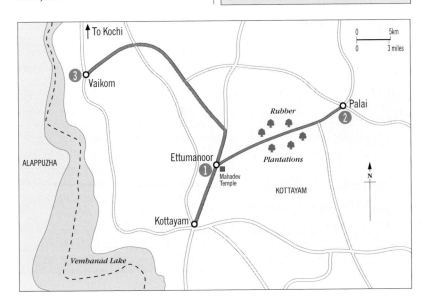

Kerala's Architecture

Although centuries of maritime contact and colonisation mean that Kerala's architecture has absorbed regional and international influences, it nevertheless retains a distinctive identity. Its distinguishing features include pagoda shapes, steeply pitched sloping roofs with gables and eaves, columned galleries and open courtyards. The main building materials are grass, clay and stone, and roofs are made of timber, terracotta tiles and thatch. Flooring is usually made from clay tiles.

In some parts of Kerala, houses are made from intricately interlocked wooden grids and panels, eschewing the use of a single nail or adhesives. The builders of Kerala follow directions for the correct construction of houses given by architectural treatises such as the *Vastu Shastra*, *Vastuvidya*, *Manushyalaya Chandrika*, *Vastupurusha Mandala* and the *Silparatna of Sri Kumara*: these provide instructions on the importance of location, the use of natural resources, and the various techniques for providing the best air flow, light and water storage.

Churches

Kerala's churches are generally European in style, with an elaborately decorated backdrop to the altar. Usually cruciform or rectangular, they have large halls for the congregation. Unlike temples, which are generally located near water sources for ritual bathing, most of the churches of Kerala have hilltop locations.

Mosques

The early mosques of Kerala were built

in the distinctive regional style, and good examples are the 16th-century mosques of Kozhikode (Calicut). In more recent times, the mosques have adopted the Middle Eastern model.

Nallakettu

The *Nallakettu*, or four-winged courtyard house, is probably the most beautiful garden dwelling in India and is certainly one of the country's finest examples of wooden architecture. It is centred around a sunken courtyard, which is designed to collect water, and also to ventilate the house with columned verandahs on all sides and galleries leading to the four blocks of the house. Guests are received in a reception room near the entrance and in a number of large halls which are used for entertainment. Louvred (dome-shaped) wooden ventilators and adjustable roofs ensure adequate airflow and light, and the layout is flexible to accommodate the addition of more rooms.

The *Ettukettu* is an extended version of the *Nallakettu*, with eight blocks enclosing the courtyard. These mansions are large, with gardens, sheds, bathing ponds, wells and granaries. The *Illam* of the Namboodri Brahmins is similar to a *Nallakettu*, but is usually more compact.

Temples

Kerala's temples are rarely taller than the trees that surround them. Entered through a gatehouse called *Gopuram*, the temple has steeply pitched roofs and the interior ceiling is usually covered with copper sheaths.

The temple clusters around the main sanctum with subsidiary shrines and the entrance hall, which is called a *mandapam*. The upper parts of the sanctuary interiors are intricately decorated with carvings or paintings to denote the importance of the *Garbagraha*, home of the deity. Most temples have a theatre called the *Kootiattum*.

Opposite: A traditional Keralan lock with intricate detail
Below: A Hindu temple wall is typically colourful and beautifully designed

Cochin

With its natural harbour and setting at the entrance to the backwaters near the Arabian Sea, Cochin's rich maritime history has left an imprint on the city's architecture. After years of maritime contact with the Arabs and the Chinese, Cochin became one of India's first European colonies, when the Portuguese settled here in the 16th century.

An ascetic on a street in Cochin

The fortunes of Cochin improved during the 16th century, when the flooding of the banks of the River Periyar created the natural harbour, while simultaneously destroying the port of Craganore that had, until then, controlled trade from central Kerala. Another stroke of luck for Cochin was the arrival of the Portuguese, who could not strike an alliance with the Zamorin, the ruler of Calicut who controlled trade between Kerala and the Middle East, and so turned their attention to Cochin. The Portuguese drew up an agreement with the Raja that helped Cochin grow in importance and at the same time allowed them to exploit its potential as a trading base. By 1663, the Portuguese lost their hold on the international spice market and the control of trade from Cochin passed to the Dutch.

Cochin received another boost in the 18th century when Dharma Raja, known as Raja Rama Varma of Kochi, introduced reforms and improved central administration. He also signed an alliance with the British East India Company that led to their taking over Cochin when subsequent generations proved incapable of handling the state's affairs.

Rice outlets are essential to trade in Cochin

When India attained independence in 1947, Cochin became one of the country's leading ports and naval bases. Today, with the twin cities of Ernakulam and Kochi, and numerous islands and peninsulas connected by bridges and ferries, Cochin expresses the eclecticism of Kerala, with Chinese fishing nets along the backwaters, European and Jewish buildings, and Hindu temples and mosques. Most of the old buildings are at Fort Kochi, a heritage zone, and in neighbouring Mattancherry, while Ernakulam is a dynamic city.

Cochin has an airport, good rail connections to most cities of India and road access to other parts of Kerala. The Government of India tourist office is at Willingdon Island, the Kerala Tourism Development Corporation is on Shanmugham Road and the District Tourism Promotion Office is at the Old Collectorate.

Bolghatty Island

The palatial mansion at Bolghatty was built in 1744 when the Dutch controlled Cochin and later became a British residency. With its acres of lawns and gardens, this old residency has been converted into a resort.

The breathtaking interior of the Mattancherry Pardesi Synagogue, rebuilt by the Dutch in the mid-17th century

Parishath Thamparam Museum

Housed in an imposing Keralan-style building, this museum has interesting temple models. Other exhibits include paintings, coins, sculptures and princely relics of Cochin state.
Darbar Hall Road, Ernakulam Tel: 2369047. 9.30am–noon & 3–5.30pm. Closed: Mon and holidays.

St Francis Church, Cochin, where Vasco da Gama was initially buried

Santa Cruz Basilica

This Roman Catholic church at Fort Kochi was built in the 16th century but had to be rebuilt in the 1800s. Notable features include the woodcarvings and murals inside. In 1984, Pope John Paul II raised the church to the status of Basilica.
Near St Francis Church.

St Francis Church

Originally dedicated to Santo Antonio, this is reputedly India's first European-built church and one of the oldest churches in southern India. Built in wood by Portuguese friars in 1503, the church was rebuilt in wood later in the same century. The oldest inscriptions found in the church are dated to 1562. Vasco da Gama was buried here in 1524, until, 14 years later, his remains were shipped to Lisbon.

Over the years the church has experienced a number of conversions and it is now used by the Church of South India. The building is impressive and an unusual feature is its rope-operated *punkah* (fan).

Mon–Sat 9.30am–5.30pm, Sun after services.

Temples

Ernakulathappan Temple in Ernakulam is known for its association with the legend of Nagarishi who was given a snake's head as a curse for killing a snake. This legend is celebrated in January with ceremonies and cultural events.

Sixteen kilometres northwest from Ernakulam is the Chottanikkara Temple, which is a popular pilgrimage site. The main deity is worshipped as Sarasvati in the morning, Bhagwati in the afternoon and Durga in the evening, and the temple is also the site of a nine-day festival in February and March.
Chottanikkara Temple receives regular buses from Ernakulam. Admission for Hindus only.

Vypeen

Vypeen Island is home to the Pallipuram Fort, which was built by the Portuguese in the 16th century and taken by the Dutch in 1663. The island also has a lighthouse, and its beaches are becoming increasingly popular with holidaymakers.

COCHIN ENVIRONS
Chennamangalam
Once the seat of the Palayathachan, hereditary ministers of Cochin Princely State, Chennamangalam has a 17th-century palace presented to them by the Dutch. The palace is now part of a trust that looks after 60 or so temples in and around the village.

The village also has interesting historical associations with the Jews, who built their oldest synagogue here (now largely in ruins), as well as with the Jesuit Christians, whose seminary was destroyed by Tipu Sultan, and the Muslims, whose 16th-century mosque still stands. Kodungallur, near Chennamangalam, is believed to be the port of Muziris mentioned by Pliny, and is also the place where St Thomas is said to have landed, bringing Christianity to Kerala. Malik Bin Dinar built Kerala's

Cochin is an excellent place to see traditional Chinese fishing nets

first mosque, Cheraman, at Kodungallur, and the mosque which now stands here probably dates from the 18th century.

Museum of Keralan History
This museum makes good use of paintings, sculptures, sound-and-light effects and audiovisual aids to depict the history of Kerala from Neolithic man through the arrival of colonial forces to the 20th century.
Open: 10am–noon & 2–4pm.
Closed: Sun. Edapally, 10km (6 miles) from Ernakulam towards Thrissur.

Tripunithura
Twelve kilometres (7.5 miles) southeast of Ernakulam, Tripunithura has the Hill Palace Museum, with its collection of coins, manuscripts, scriptures and princely relics of Cochin and Travancore.
Open: 9am–12.30pm, & 2–4pm.
Closed: Sun. Small admission charge.
Hill Palace Museum, Tripunithura, Chottanikkara Road.

CHINESE FISHING NETS

Chinese fishing nets were probably introduced when Kerala traded with the Chinese court. The nets are framed with wood and strung along poles that can be 3m (10ft) long, tied to suspended boulders. The boulders help keep the net down when it is dipped into the water at high tide. Four or five men pull the net out of the water using a rope with a pulley system and rocks at the other end to balance the weight. The nets bring in large catches, and a good place to see them in action is at Kochi.

Walk: Mattancherry

This walk through Mattancherry, near Fort Kochi, offers an opportunity to see Cochin Synagogue, the royal palace and the Jew Town Market, a spice trade centre.

Start at the Mattancherry Palace, which has good road and ferry access to the rest of Cochin.

Allow 4 hours, including time for shopping.

1 Mattancherry Palace

Also called the Dutch Palace, this palace was actually built by the Portuguese in the 16th century and gifted to their ally, the ruler of Cochin, who gave them trading rights. The palace was completely renovated and practically rebuilt after the Dutch took over Cochin in 1663. Built on two floors around a quadrangle, the palace incorporates European influences into the traditional

Nallakettu plan (*see pp100–101*). It has a Bhagvati Temple in the central courtyard and Shiva and Vishnu Temples to the south.

The palace has a museum of princely relics, but is known mainly for its marvellous murals depicting the entire Ramayana and scenes from the Mahabharata dating from the 16th and 17th centuries. The Central Hall was used for coronation ceremonies and has

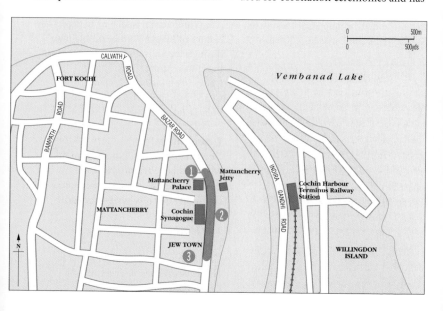

an interesting display of dresses, turbans and palanquins. In other rooms there are portraits of the Rajas from 1864 to 1964, weapons including ceremonial swords, costumes and other princely memorabilia.

From the main gate of the Mattancherry Palace, head left for a few hundred metres and then left again for the synagogue.

2 Cochin Synagogue

Also called the Mattancherry Pardesi Synagogue, this was founded in 1568 and rebuilt by the Dutch in 1664, two years after the Portuguese destroyed the building. A wealthy Jewish merchant, Ezekial Rahabi, donated the clock tower in the 18th century.

Notable features include the Cantonese willow-pattern tiles, Belgian chandeliers, interlocking pews, a ladies' gallery supported by gilt columns, ornate brass pulpit and a slab from the 14th-century Kochangadi Synagogue that is now in ruins. An elaborate Ark has scrolls from the Jewish *Torah* (the first five books of the Hebrew Bible), and gifts of gold crowns from the princely family of Cochin.

Turn left from the synagogue and then left again for the pepper exchange, established to fuel foreign investment into the spice trade. The pepper exchange marks the start of the Jew Town Market.

3 Jew Town

The market has developed into a bazaar for antiques, curios, handicrafts and tourist souvenirs, with shops selling anything from Kathakali masks, jewel boxes and trinkets to ornate bullock carts.

From Jew Town turn left on the road along the waterfront to return to the Mattancherry Palace, or to take the ferry out from the Mattancherry Jetty.

JEWRY OF COCHIN

In Jew Town you are likely to hear stories about Jews who arrived here in King Solomon's ships about the 9th century BC, those who arrived in Kerala fleeing Babylon in the 6th century BC, those who arrived from Assyria in search of refuge, as well as those who migrated to Kerala after the destruction of Jerusalem in the 1st century AD and the 10,000 Jews who fled from Palestine in the 2nd century and were allowed to settle at Muziris (probably Kodungallur).

Ideal go-betweens for the local Malayalam population and overseas traders, Jews became one of Kerala's most influential communities.

Raja Bhaskara Ravi Varma, who ruled in the 10th and 11th centuries, granted the Jewish community the village of Anjuvaddam and its surrounding land. By the 16th century the Arabs and Portuguese had all but destroyed the Jewish community in Kerala, who then moved to Cochin and were granted protection, land and titles. Their population was augmented by those fleeing persecution in Europe.

The Jewish population dwindled with the mass migration to Israel in the 20th century, and today only a few Jewish families live in Cochin.

Thrissur

Thrissur is an abbreviation of Thiru, Shiva and Perur, meaning, 'the city named after Lord Shiva', and for centuries it has been an important religious and cultural centre. Widely regarded as Kerala's cultural capital, Thrissur District is famous for its temples, churches, arts colleges and training schools for the performing arts.

A temple elephant housed at Punnathur Kotha, Guruvayoor

The imposing Indo-European façade of Lourdes Cathedral

Located at the western end of the Palakad Gap, or Palghat Pass, Thrissur formed a vital link between the coast and the interior of the peninsula. The Rajas of Central Kerala reigned from here before moving their capital to Cochin. Thrissur fell to the Zamorin of Malabar, then Sultan Hyder Ali, and eventually to the European colonial powers.

Thrissur has good road and rail connections to Thiruvananthapuram, Kozhikode and Cochin. The tourist information offices are at the Government Guest House and near the Town Hall.

Lourdes Cathedral

This cathedral has an impressive Indo-European façade with pink spires. The interior of the cathedral has an attractive underground shrine.

About 1km (0.5 mile) out of town centre towards Peechi.

Vadakkunnathan Temple

Traditionally this temple on a hillock is regarded as the centre of Thrissur, with roads radiating on all sides. The temple is an excellent example of Kerala's architecture, with fine woodcarvings decorating the roof and façade. Predominantly a Shiva Temple, it also has shrines to other deities. The main sanctuaries are dedicated to Shiva as Vadakkunnathan, and to Sankara Narayan, with a Ganesh shrine between them. The interior has beautiful murals near the main shrines. Entry is for Hindus only, but visitors are usually allowed on special days, including the famous Pooram Festival.

Open: 4–10.30am & 5–8.30pm.

THRISSUR ENVIRONS
Angamali

This is an important Syrian Christian centre and it was once home to one of

Vaddukkannathan Temple may be admired for its architecture and detailed woodcarvings

Temple offerings at Guruvayoor temple

the most important bishoprics in Kerala. Nearby, at Akaparambhu, the church of Mar Sabore and Afroth was founded in the 9th century, although the present structure dates from after the 16th century and shows some Portuguese influences. It is particularly noted for its murals narrating stories from the Bible. *On National Highway 47 to Ernakulam.*

Guruvayoor

Guruvayoor is an important religious centre for the worship of the infant Krishna. According to one of the legends associated with the temple, the site was selected by Guru, preceptor of the gods, and Vayu, lord of the winds, when they met Lord Shiva and Parvati with Parsurama, creator of Kerala, at the tank of Guruvayoor. The tank has a statue of Krishna playing the flute. The temple has carved columns, a tall gold flagpost, called the *dhvajastambha*, a lamp tower, some murals and the image of a four-armed Krishna with a conch, a discus, a mace and a lotus.

The 16th-century poet Narayana Bhattatiri wrote the famous Hindu text, *Narayaneeyam* (inspired by the Bhagwad), at Guruvayoor. A sufferer of rheumatic illness, he was cured during his visit to Guruvayoor, and since then the temple is regularly visited by people with rheumatism seeking recovery through the blessings of the infant Krishna. The temple is also a popular location for marriage ceremonies.

The temple elephants are housed at the Punnathur Kotha, an old fortified complex. This is a good place for the elephants being bathed by the *mahouts*, but visitors must be careful, as the animals can be dangerous, especially the males during the breeding season. Wild elephants are brought here to be tamed for the temple festivals. *Regular buses from Thrissur to the bus station east of the temple.*

Irinjalakuda

Irinjalakuda's Natana Kairali Research and Performing Centre is dedicated to the performance, preservation, documentation and promotion of Kerala's performing arts, particularly Kuttiyam, Nangiar Koothu and puppetry. Performances are held here from time to time, especially during the centre's 12-day annual festival.

The Koodal Manikhyam Temple at Irinjalakuda is an unusual temple dedicated to Rama's brother Bharata, and depicting his joy when he learned of the victory of Rama and his reunion with Sita. Irinjalakuda is also home to the Church of St Thomas, an impressive building erected in 1917 on the site of an older church which was built here in 1845. In January the images of saints are taken out in procession, accompanied by firework displays.

Regular buses from Thrissur.
For information about courses at Natana Kairali Research & Performing Centre for Traditional Arts contact the director at Venu G, Natana Kairali, Ammanur Chakyar Madhom, Irinjalakuda 680121.
Tel: 0488 2825559.
venuji@satyam.net

Kalady

Kalady, by the River Periyar, is the birthplace of Sankaracharya, one of the most important philosophers in India. In the 8th century, Sankaracharya founded the Advainta Vendanta, which has spread throughout southern India and to other parts of the country. Kalady has two shrines in his memory, as well as a tower with details about his life and the Advainta ways of worship.

Kerala Kalamandalam

Founded in the 1920s and 1930s by the poet Vellathol Menon and his associate Mukunda Raja, this is an important academy for teaching the performing arts of Kerala, particularly Kathakali, Mohiniattam, Kuttiyattam and Onam Thullal. The centre is credited with the revival of Kerala's dance forms and for opening its doors to Hindus and non-Hindus alike, and it has also established international links for the promotion of Kathakali overseas. Located in Cheruthuruthy, a village on the shores of River Bharatpuzha, the campus's pleasant buildings include a theatre which is designed in the style of the performing halls of Kerala's temples.
Visiting hours are 9am–noon & 2–5pm on working days, and the office can give information on the various performances and courses on offer.
For interaction with the masters and for information on courses at Kerala Kalamandalam write to the secretary.
info@kalamandalam.com

Megalith sites

Huge stone monuments are among the earliest evidences of settlement in Kerala. Some of the best megalithic sites are located near Guruvayoor, while Chovannur has a sizeable number of the 'hat-stones' (locally called *topi-kals*) that are distinctive Iron-Age megalithic remains. Substantial remnants of Kerala's megalithic era can also be seen at Porkalam.

Music and Dance

Kathakali

The dance drama of Kathakali is recognised as one of the major classical Indian dance styles. The main elements of Kathakali are the sung narrative, the accompaniment of percussion instruments and the danced mime. The performer uses a variety of gestures and steps to portray the narrative, which is sung as the background theme of the performance. Boys are recruited at a very young age and spend seven or more years learning the *mudras*, hand and finger gestures and movements of

the neck, head, tongue, eyes, feet, toes, arms and hands.

Mohiniattam, the dance of the enchantress, is a sensuous solo female performance that evokes the mood of love. The dance is dedicated to the female incarnation of Vishnu, Mohini the enchantress, who gives pleasure to the virtuous and brings destruction to the immoral.

Ottan Thulal is a male solo performance that depicts topical issues. Its simplicity, humour and satire have made it a popular art in Kerala, and it is performed at public places such as marketplaces and temple platforms. The script is usually drawn from epics or popular stories which are blended with topical repartee to create a spoof on the current political scene or on bureaucracy. The dancer enacts the script with gestures, movements and expression.

Koothu, a solo performance, and Koothiattam (sometimes spelt Koodiattam), a group performance, are ancient Sanskrit dramas believed to be the inspiration behind the growth of dance dramas like Kathakali in Kerala. The Krishnanattam, patronised by the Raja Manaveda, the Zamorin of Kozhikode in the mid-17th century, has become a ritual dance at the Krishna temple of Guruvayoor, enacting the life of Krishna. Ramanattam is a similar performance, dedicated to the life of Rama.

Ritual dances can still be witnessed in the temples of Kerala. Teyyam dancers are elaborately dressed and vividly made up, and the dance, together with its accompanying music, evokes the temple deity to protect people from disease and harm. The dance ends with the performers taking on a trance-like appearance. This dance is popular in north Kerala, especially in Kannur and Kasaragode districts, and along the southern Konkan coast.

Mutiyettu is the ritual dance enacting the Puranic tale, Darika-Vadha, which deals with the battle between Goddess Kali and demon Darika. The Patayani (sometimes pronounced Padayani) presents the wrathful appearance of Bhagwati, a manifestation of Goddess Kali. This dance is performed in central Kerala, where people believe it has magical properties and keeps evil spirits away from their homes and crops. Kummathakali, yet another performance dealing with tales of Goddess Kali, is a folk dance seen in temples of Thrissur and Palakkad, specially the former, during Onam. The highlight of the performance is the brightly coloured masks worn by the dancers. Tiruvatirakali, also called Kaikottikali, is performed by women as a symbol of marital peace.

Opposite: The mesmeric costumes and dramatic dancing style of Kathakali make such performances highly memorable

Periyar

Periyar Wildlife Reserve is one of Kerala's most popular tourist destinations. The reserve's artificial lake was created in 1895 by British engineers, in order to irrigate Madurai and Ramanathapuram districts and to provide water to the city of Madurai. The dam submerged prime forests but resulted in the Maharaja of Travancore protecting the richly vegetated hills adjoining the lake.

Cruise boats convey visitors to the Periyar Wildlife Reserve

Periyar is 110km (69 miles) from Cochin. There is a tourist information office at Aranya Niwas in the park, and the wildlife officer at Thekkadi can be contacted for details about viewing facilities.

Periyar Wildlife Reserve

This sanctuary was established by the Travancore State in 1934 and became part of 'Project Tiger' in 1973. Although Periyar is a tiger reserve, it is more famous for its elephants, which can be seen from the tourist launches which operate two-hour trips on the lake. Elephants come to the lake to drink and to feed on the marshy grasslands. Gaur (Indian bison), sambar, wild boar and Nilgiri langur are common sightings, and lucky visitors may also see sloth bear, dhole (wild dog), otters and the endangered lion-tailed macaque. This is a good spot for birdwatching, with species such as darter, cormorant, osprey, stork and kingfisher.

Guided nature treks depart from the information centre and last about three hours. On these treks you are likely to see barking deer, Malabar giant squirrels, monkeys such as langur and bonnet macaques, great and grey hornbills, grey jungle fowl, mynahs, orioles, racket-tailed drongos and monitor lizards. Some tourists come face to face with elephant herds, and watchtowers and viewing platforms can also be used, for a fee.

More serious treks, such as the Tiger Trails (an eco-development project), are also possible and include camping and staying at watchtowers in the forests. These treks cover habitats like the grasslands, where the mega-herbivores are usually seen, the moist deciduous forests and the semi-evergreen and evergreen forests. Tiger and panther sightings are rare, but visitors can see a number of other mammals, as well as an interesting variety of birds and butterflies.

Two-hour launch cruises, called boat safaris, depart from the jetty at regular intervals. The first morning cruise runs from 7–9am, and the last from 4–6pm. The guided nature trek starts at 7am.

Plantations

Some spice plantations near Periyar Tiger Reserve welcome visitors, and tourist offices, spice shops and some hotels run guided tours to the

cardamom, rubber and coffee plantations of Murikkady, the pepper plantations at Vandiperiyar and the cardamom centre at Vandanmedu. Peermade (sometimes spelt Pirmed), on the road from Kottayam to Kumily leading to Periyar Tiger Reserve, has a number of picturesquely located tea, rubber and cardamon plantations.
Most hotels and resorts at Thekkady, Kumily , Vandanmedu and Pirmed can arrange visits to plantations.

Temples

There are a number of temples near Periyar Tiger Reserve. One of the best known is Mangaladevi Temple, situated on the crest of a hill, but it is now largely neglected and is only open for certain festivals. Permission is required from the forest department office at Thekkadi to visit this temple.
Wildlife Preservation Officer, Periyar Tiger Reserve, PO Kumily, Thekkady. Tel: 0486-2322027.

Elephants roam freely around the Wildlife Reserve

In the minds of most travellers, the Indian elephant is inseparable from Kerala. Tuskers are invariably male, although there are also tuskless males called *makhnas*, while females have small tusks that are either not visible or protrude only a few inches. Elephants usually associate in mixed groups that could range from a few individuals to large herds of more than 60. Mature bulls generally move away from the herd, except for the occasional grazing session or to mate. These solitary males have a tendency to charge when disturbed, especially when they are in 'musth' – a period of excitement which is usually associated with the desire for a mate – so they must be viewed from a safe distance. Elephants are most active in the early morning and late evening. They wander over a large area and wild ones are often seen outside the wildlife reserves.

Periyar in Kerala is one of the premier tiger reserves of south India, and many other sanctuaries and national parks of

Kerala have resident tiger populations, but few visitors actually spot them. Tigers often take to the water and have been seen swimming at Periyar lake. The leopard or panther is more abundant than the tiger in India, but, being even more elusive, is rarely seen. Its ability to climb has given the panther a varied diet, from monkeys to deer, and panthers sometimes come down to villages to hunt dogs and livestock. Indian panthers are usually buff-grey and white in colour, dotted with

solid spots on the head and black rosettes on the rest of the body, but some are entirely black. The lesser cats, such as the jungle cat, forest dwelling leopard and fishing cat, have longer legs than domestic cats. Civets are related to cats but easily distinguished by their long bodies, elongated skull, pointed muzzle, short legs and long tail. The hyena, contrary to popular belief, is not a dog but a relative of cats and civets. The Indian mongoose is a common sight in Kerala but other species – the brown mongoose and the ruddy mongoose, for example – can also be seen in the forests.

The tawny and bushy tailed *dhole*, or Indian wild dog, is one of the most dreaded predators, despite its diminutive size, because it hunts in a pack and pursues its prey relentlessly. Jackals are better known as scavengers than predators and are often seen near habitations, while the Indian fox is smaller than a jackal and is usually seen in open country. The sloth bear lives in forests where it can forage for enough fruit, honey, termites and so on, to maintain its massive body.

Herbivores include the endangered Nilgiri tahr, gaur, sambar (the largest Indian deer), the spotted chital deer, barking deer and the rabbit-sized mouse deer. The most commonly seen monkeys are the bonnet macaque and hanuman langur, while the Nilgiri langur, lion-tailed macaque and the nocturnal loris inhabit the forests.

Striped palm squirrels are among India's most common animals, and Kerala is also home to giant and flying squirrels, as well as porcupines, hares and several species of bat.

Opposite: Bath time!
Above: A chital (spotted deer) at Nagarhole, near Wayanad

M u n n a r

At 1652m (5507ft), Munnar has developed into a hill resort for visitors to Kerala. It is a small town with a spectacular setting near Annamudi, South India's highest peak. The abbreviation of two Tamil words, *moonu* (three) and *aar* (river), Munnar lies at the confluence of Kuthirappuzh, Nallathanni and Kundala.

Tea picking at Munnar

Munnar is 304km (190 miles) from Thiruvananthapuram, 153km (96 miles) from Cochin and 287km (179 miles) from Kozhikode.

Like other hill stations of India, the small town of Munnar was discovered and established by the British to serve the needs of some of the world's highest tea plantations. Until the late 19th century, Munnar was a deeply forested area inhabited mainly by tribal groups like the Madhuvans.

The growth of Munnar as the commercial centre of tea estates began in 1887 with the opening of the High Ranges of Travancore, also called the Kannan Devan Hills, for agriculture. An official of Travancore, Munro, was the first to lease the hill tracts for agriculture. After experimenting with rubber, chichona and other crops, the planters found the area suitable for the cultivation of tea. The giant tea company of James Finlay & Co was established in 1895 and eventually controlled most of the tea estates around Munnar. Access to Munnar was by train from Tamil Nadu, until 1931 when a road was opened from Cochin, making life easier for the planters.

In 1964, the Finlay estates went into a joint venture with the Tatas, one of India's wealthiest families. Today, Tata Tea controls most of the tea production around Munnar and is among the largest producers in India. The tea from their Kanan Devan Estate is especially famous.

Munnar still has colonial buildings, including old bungalows, and recreational life is focused around the clubs which were set up for British planters.

A priest and tea plantation workers perform Hindu rites

Christchurch

This Protestant church, built in 1910, is set on a hill near the town centre. It has a pleasant interior which is notable for its stained-glass windows, and its original pews can still be seen. The cemetery on the hillside above the church is older, with tombs dating from 1894 and brass plaques in honour of the planters.

This church is in Old Munnar and has services in Tamil and Malayalam. The Christmas mass is popular.

Devikulam

15km (9 miles) from Munnar town, Devikulam has beautiful views over the high ranges of the Western Ghats.

Devikulam Lake is in a private estate and you will need permission from the Tata office at Munnar to visit it.

The lake is particularly beautiful, and locals believe that Sita bathed at the lake, and so they consider it to be holy. The name Devikulam means 'the lake of the goddess'.

Mount Carmel Church

Father Alphonse, who came to Munnar from Spain in 1854, established the first Catholic chapel in the High Ranges in Old Munnar in 1898. The present Mount Carmel Church was built in 1938 and consecrated by the bishop of Vijayapuram.

On the road to Tata Gen Hospital.

Packing up the tea for processing at Munnar

Tour: Munnar to Top Station

Most visitors to Munnar come to explore the surrounding hills with their neatly manicured tea estates and forests. One of the prettiest routes is the drive from Munnar to Top Station, with its high-altitude tea estates, as well as flowering plants such as Neelukurunji, an orchid that blooms every 12 years, covering the mountain sides with colour.

Although the distance from Munnar to Top Station is only about 34km (21 miles), you need to allow 4–5 hours for the return trip, as the mountain roads are slow-going. It is also a good idea to check on the road conditions before setting off: during the rainy season fallen trees are not uncommon.

Take the road from Munnar to Top Station, leading past tea estates, some of which have retail outlets. It may be possible to obtain permission to visit one of the tea estates and see a working factory. Plantation activities such as tea picking can be seen from the road on working days.

1 Mattupetty Lake

At an altitude of 1,700m (5,667ft), this huge lake was created by a hydroelectric project. It has been developed as a tourist attraction, and facilities include speedboat rides and horse riding. Elephants and wild boar are sometimes seen in the surrounding forests.
3km (1.9 miles) after Mattupetty, you will see the entrance of the Indo-Swiss dairy project, which is now run by the Kerala Livestock Development Board as a cattle breeding and research centre. From here the road rises to Kundaly.

2 Kundaly

The dam at Kundaly is a few hundred metres off the road. Full of trout and other fish, it has a beautiful setting in the hills and is surrounded by

The lush landscape near Munnar

grasslands and forests, where elephant and gaur (Indian bison) can sometimes be spotted. An old colonial inspection bungalow stands in the woods near the lakeshores. 4km (2.5 miles) from the dam is a golf course, with an attractive clubhouse, administered by Tata Tea for planters and guests. Permission is required for a visit or a game and the last stretch of road requires a jeep.
After Kundaly, the road ascends to Top Station.

3 Top Station

At 2,200m (7,333ft), Top Station, on the border of Tamil Nadu, has a great view of some of India's highest tea plantations. Little now remains of the ropeway that was used to transport tea to the valley floor, called Lower Station.

From Top Station you can return to Munnar. Some travellers may wish to use this route to travel on to Kodaikanal, a hill station in Tamil Nadu.

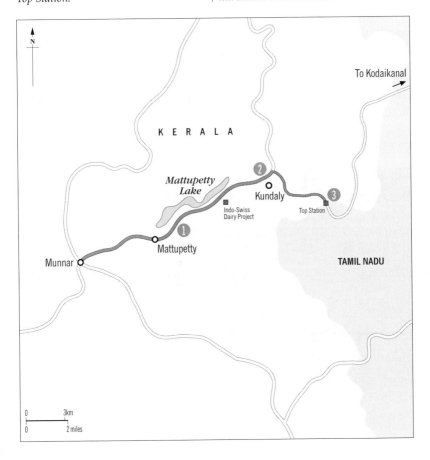

Tour: Wildlife Trail from Munnar to Chinnar

The 60-km (37.5-mile) route from Munnar to Chinnar Wildlife Sanctuary, at the Tamil Nadu border, is great for seeing a variety of endangered flora and fauna from the sandalwood tree to the Nilgiri tahr.

Take the road north from Munnar to Rajmalai, and turn left from the main road about 14km (8.75 miles) from Munnar. This is a full-day tour and an early start is necessary as the roads are hilly, and some walking is involved at Rajmalai, Marayoor and Chinnar.

1 Rajmalai

Rajmalai has the only permissible path for visitors in the Eravikulam National Park, home of the endangered Nilgiri tahr. A relative of the domestic goat, the Nilgiri tahr has erect ears, long sturdy limbs and rounded horns that end in an impressive curving sweep. It does not have the beard and twisted horns of a goat, but it is just as agile and sure-footed.

Designated a national park in 1978, Eravikulam was previously set up as a sanctuary for the protection of the Nilgiri tahr. Spanning an area of 97km (61 miles) of *shola* habitat, comprising rolling grassland and forest, the park contains the high peak of Mt Annamudi. Besides Nilgiri tahr, Eravikulam is also the home of elephant, tiger, panther, wild dog, Nilgiri langur, lion-tailed macaque and giant squirrel. From the gate of Rajmalai, the steep path leads to the Tata Tea Estate, which affords good opportunities to see the

A bonnet macaque monkeying around at Chinnar Wildlife Sanctuary

Nilgiri tahr and a variety of birds.
Return to the highway and drive north past tea estates and Hindu shrine. To the left of the highway is Marayoor village.

2 Marayoor

This natural sandalwood forest is the only substantial one left in Kerala, and it is strictly protected. Only dead and diseased trees are removed. The forest officer may be able to arrange treks with Tamil tribal guides. Marayoor has important megalith sites and prehistoric rock paintings, but be warned that the trek to this particular site is strenuous.
From Marayoor, the road continues 20km (12.5 miles) to Chinnar Wildlife Sanctuary. Langur, bonnet macaque and peafowl are often seen from the road. Just off the main road is a watchtower, which is great for viewing wildlife.

3 Chinnar

Chinnar was declared a wildlife sanctuary in 1984 and contains a range of habitats from *shola* forest and grasslands in the hills to drier forests in the rain shadow region. This 90-sq km (56-sq mile) reserve has elephant, gaur, deer and panther, as well as the rare grizzled giant squirrel which is hard to spot. A good variety of birds and butterflies can be seen along the path to the watchtower.
The drive from the entrance of Chinnar Wildlife Sanctuary to Munnar is 58km (36 miles), but expect to spend 3–4 hours on the road. Although it is tempting to make a late start from Chinnar, this is not advisable because animals are active in the evening, and the presence of tuskers could give rise to some potentially dangerous situations.

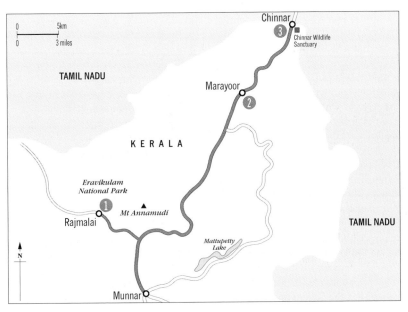

Kozhikode

Kozhikode, or Calicut, is one of the cities most associated with the spice trade. Mentioned in the writings of Marco Polo, Kozhikode was ruled by a dynasty with the title Zamorin, which means 'king of the seas'. The Zamorin had strong alliances with the Arabs, giving them a monopoly over the spice trade.

Sampling the rice at a wholesale shop in Kozhikode

The Zamorins were also patrons of the arts and of culture in general, and Kozhikode became famous for its textiles (calico is said to derive from Calicut, the colonial name of the city). In the 15th century, the power of the Zamorins covered about half of Kerala.

The balance of fortunes between the Zamorin and other rulers of Kerala changed when Vasco da Gama discovered an alternative route to Kerala from Europe which broke the Arab monopoly over trade westward from India. Vasco da Gama's fleet is said to have landed at Kappad near Kozhikode in 1498. Unsuccessful in forging links with the Zamorin, he turned his attention to Cochin. Seeing the alliance between the Dutch and the Cochin Raja as a threat to their trade monopoly, the Zamorin set out to conquer Cochin, but the Portuguese intervened and made Cochin their protectorate. The Zamorins survived two Portuguese attacks, although one severely damaged Kozhikode, and they eventually made peace with the Portuguese in order to remain contenders in the spice market. Sultan Hyder Ali conquered Kozhikode from the Zamorin, and his son Tipu ruled it for some time. Later, the British vanquished the Sultans and took

control of Malabar, making it a province of their Madras Presidency in 1800.

Kozhikode was a centre for rebellions against British rule, beginning when the British administration made laws that supported the landlords rather than the farmers. The Indian National Congress found enthusiastic support in the Malabar province, and the death of prisoners being transported in a railway carriage triggered a rebellion in 1921.

Today, Kozhikode is a commercial centre of Kerala's northern districts and an important centre for the timber trade and for boat building. Known for its old Moplah and Nair houses, Kozhikode has also experienced much new building activity in recent years.

Kozhikode is 382km (239 miles) from Thiruvananthapuram and 188km (118 miles) from Cochin, with good road and rail connections. It also has an international airport.

Mananchira

Little remains of the Zamorin's old royal enclave at Mananchira. Locals believe the Zamorin killed himself in his palace, rather than face defeat at the hands of the Mysorian Sultans after peace talks failed. Temples, mosques and churches surround the square.

Mosques
The Kuttichara area of Kozhikode is known for its medieval mosques. The four-storey Mishkal Mosque is in the traditional Kerala style, with gabled roof and wooden columns; partly burned by the Portuguese in 1510, most of the original building still stands. Another mosque in the traditional style is the Muccunti Palli, which has a slab stating that the land was a donation from the Zamorin.

The mosques are walking distance from one another.

Museums
The Pazhassirajah Museum has interesting models of different kinds of megalithic monuments of Kerala and replicas of Hindu temples, as well as collections of coins, bronzes and copies of original murals. Next door, the Krishna Menon Museum has clothes, speeches and photographs of this former defence minister of India, while the Art Gallery in the same building has an excellent collection of paintings by Indian artists, including Raja Varma.
The museums are on East Hill about 5km (3 miles) from the city centre.
Timings for the museums: 10am–12.30pm & 2.30–5.00pm. Closed: Mon and on Wed morning.

Tali Temple
This temple is known for its woodcarvings and huge statues of the deities. Probably dating from the reign of the Zamorin, it is now an important religious centre in Kozhikode.
The temple is south of the city centre.

Wind-drying a sari on Kappad Beach

KOZHIKODE ENVIRONS
Beypore
The coastal centre of Beypore, 8km (5 miles) south of Kozhikode, is believed to have been a shipbuilding centre for many centuries. Today, its yards produce hand-built dhows called *urus*, which are exported to the Gulf countries. These huge vessels can weigh 700 tonnes (689 long tons) or more. The yard owners also make smaller boats, including miniature replicas of the *urus* for visitors. Anchors are sold at Beypore, known for its Tasara Creative Weaving Centre which trains artisans in textile skills.

Kadalundi Bird Sanctuary
This bird sanctuary at the estuary of the Kadalundi River has a number of resident species of kingfishers, herons and gulls. It is best visited in winter when flocks of migrants come here. *The sanctuary is on two sides of the river about 19km (12 miles) from Kozhikode.*

Kappad
Kappad, about 16km (10 miles) north of Kozhikode, has a stone memorial marking the spot where Vasco da Gama is said to have landed in 1498. The beach at Kappad is popular with day trippers from Kozhikode, as the city's own beaches are rather crowded.

Kottakal
Kottakal is home to the Arya Vaidya Sala Hospital, which is regarded as one of India's most renowned Ayurvedic

Muslim women and children wait at a bus stop in Kozhikode

The Vasco da Gama memorial pillar at Kappad

centres, and which has been involved in research and practice for more than 100 years.
48km (30 miles) from Kozhikode. Arya Vaidya Sala, Kottakal. Tel: 0493-2742216.

Mahe

Mahe has an interesting colonial history, first under the British and then as a French colony under Pondicherry. The French arrived at Malabar in the 17th century to establish its spice-trading base. Located on a hill and overlooking a river, the town was named after Mahe de Labourdonnais who conquered the town in 1725. Handed over to the Government of India in 1958, Mahe has few remnants of its French colonial history, one exception being St Theresa's Church. The town also has an arts institution, the Malayala Kalagramam Centre for Arts and Ideas, which offers courses in music, dance, sculpture and painting.
60km (37 miles) from Kozhikode towards Kannur. For information about courses contact Malayala Kala. Tel: 0490-2332961.

Vadakara

The Lokarnarkavu Temple Complex is 5km (3 miles) from the town centre of Vadakara. It has three temples, with the oldest and biggest dedicated to Durga and the others to Vishnu and Shiva, as well as a number of rock caves and tanks. The temples have attractive carvings near the entrance and some interesting paintings inside.
Vadakara is on National Highway 17.

Kannur

Kannur, or Cannanore, was an important spice-trading port, visited by the likes of Marco Polo. Ruled for centuries by the Kolatri Rajas, European powers began to exert their influence from the 15th century. The Portuguese made it a military base, building a fort which took advantage of Kannur's position on raised ground above cliffs facing the sea.

The fishing fleet haul in the nets at Kannur

After a period of Dutch rule, Kannur became an important British centre in 1790. Besides the buildings erected by the Europeans, it also has some old quarters of the local Moplah (Mapilla) Muslim trading community.

Kannur is 278km (174 miles) from Cochin, 90km (56 miles) from Kozhikode and 465km (291 miles) from Thiruvananthapuram, with good rail connections to these cities, and to Mumbai, Delhi and other major Indian cities.

Beaches

Kannur has a number of beaches, although none of them is particularly well known as a tourist destination. The most popular is Payyambalam Beach, near the fort.

St Angelo Fort

This fort was built by the Portuguese in 1505 during the Viceregalship of Almeida. The Dutch occupied the fort in 1663 and sold it in 1772 to the Ali Raja of Kannur, who was the first Muslim ruler of Kerala. Ali Raja had a short tenure, before the British conquest of 1790 made St Angelo Fort one of the most important British army bases in South India. Built from laterite blocks, the fort walls are protected by the sea, and by a moat on the landward side. The British practically rebuilt the rest of the fort within the walls for their garrisons, and some of the old cannons still stand, but the highlight of a visit to the fort is the view of the sea, and occasionally of the fishing fleet returning with their catch.

The impressive St Angelo Fort was built by the Portuguese at the turn of the 16th century

KANNUR ENVIRONS
Chirakkal
This was the capital of the Kolatri Rajas when they ruled Kannur, and the wooden mansion that served as their palace can be seen here. Chirakkal also has some interesting temples facing a huge tank.

Parsinidakavu Temple
This temple rises on the banks of the Valapatanam and is associated with the legend of Muthapan, the hunter form of Lord Shiva, who is said to have appeared before (or been born) to a Shiva-worshipping childless landlord couple. As a hunter, Muthapan did not appeal to the landlord family, so Shiva appeared before them in his divine form. He was fond of toddy, and was given it whenever he was called upon to perform a miracle, which is why toddy remains the main offering at the temple.

The non-conformist temple has always been open to all castes, and to non-Hindus as well. The main tourist attraction is to attend the dawn and dusk Teyyam performance (*see pp112–13*) which opens and closes the temple ceremonies. The Teyyam here portrays the legend of Muthapan, said to have selected Parsinidakavu as his sacred home. Muthapan is depicted with a dog as a companion, and therefore street dogs are welcome into the temple and are offered toddy and fish.
The temple is about 18km (11 miles) from Kannur.

Thoddikulam Temple
This temple, east of Kannur off the road from Thalasseri to Mananthvadi, is known for its beautiful murals which are believed to date from the 16th century.
The temple is about 25km (15.5 miles) east of Thalasseri (see pp134–5).

A Teyyam dance performance at the Parsinidakavu Temple

Tour: Kannur District's Cottage Industries

Called the 'Land of Loom and Lore', Kannur is known for its handloom weaving. This tour visits two of Kerala's best-known cooperatives, as well as the spice plantation at Anjarakandy which is a large producer of cinnamon.
Allow 4 hours for the tour, including travel time.

Take the National Highway south from Kannur and then turn onto the state road to Mysore. After about 10km (6 miles) you will come to one of the units of the Kerala Dinesh Beedi Workers' Cooperative.

1 Kerala Dinesh Beedi Workers' Cooperative

Here you can see workers making *beedis*, the local cigarettes that are popular in India. Owned and managed by the workers and retirees, most of them women, the government supports the cooperative's aims, which are to improve the income of *beedi* workers and to give them better working conditions than elsewhere. Most of the workers are 'rollers', who cut the leaves before filling them with tobacco and rolling them into reefers. The *beedis* are then tied into bundles and sent to the packing and shipping departments.

Deft finger work at the Dinesh Beedi Workers' Cooperative

An important feature of the unit, embodying the literacy and political awareness of the people of Kerala, is the 'reader' who reads aloud from the local newspapers so that the workers can hear. Although the cooperative has been successful in improving the conditions of Kerala's *beedi*-workers, and has sustained profitability for most of the years of operation, it now faces the challenge of diversification with the decline in tobacco consumption.

It is working on other projects, such as agro-processing, for which most of the workers are being trained in making and packaging curry powders, pickles, coconut cream, jams and other popular food products. A more ambitious project is the cooperative's move into information technology, which has established training centres for a number of high-tech applications.

Approximately 4km (2.5 miles) further along on the Kannur to Mysore Road is the Kanjhirode Weavers' Cooperative.

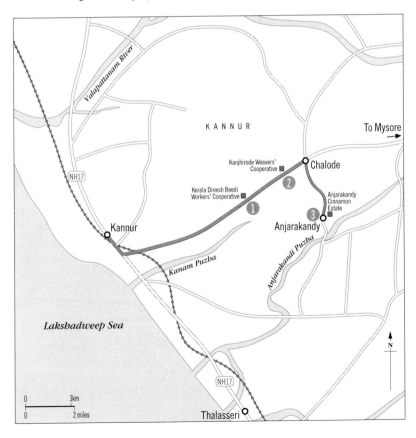

Woven fabrics at the Kanjhirode Weavers' Cooperative

2 Kanjhirode Weavers' Cooperative

Kannur is known as the 'land of loom and lore' and about 70,000 residents of Kannur are employed by handloom cooperatives. The Kanjhirode Weavers' Cooperative Society alone employs around 400 people in its factories, about half of them women. The cooperative was established in 1952 and has also taken initiative for setting up a common facilities centre and dye house for units in the district for cotton and silk weaving. There is a retail outlet that sells products like shirts, fabrics, furnishings, sarees and sarongs. It has sustained reasonably high profitability and exports much of its production. Visitors can ask permission to see the various processes, from spinning and weaving to dyeing. The cooperative uses different kinds of looms, including a 229-cm (90-inch) Malabar loom.

For guided tours of the factory call the secretary of the cooperative at 0497-2851259.

Continue east to Chalode and turn right on the road to Thalasseri for Anjarakandy.

3 Anjarakandy Cinnamon Estate

This is one of the largest cinnamon estates in Asia, covering about 150 acres (61 hectares). Established in 1767 by the East India Company, it was a mixed plantation of cinnamon, pepper, cloves, nutmeg and other spices, but it now specialises in cinnamon.

Visitors can see the processes of preparing the cinnamon spice and extracting oil for perfume.

From Anjarakandy, roads connect to the highway between Kannur and Thalasseri (see pp134–5).

Working a loom at the Weavers' Cooperative

Tour: Kannur to Thalasseri

This tour covers the attractions on National Highway 17 between Kannur and Thalasseri, known for their forts.
Take National Highway 17 south from Kannur to Thalasseri. Five kilometres (3 miles) before Thalasseri is Muzhapalingau Beach. Allow about 4–5 hours for the return trip.

1 Muzhapalingau Beach

This is one of the finest beaches in Kerala, stretching for 4km (2.5 miles) along a bay with a wide strip of white sand. The palm trees to the north and the rocks to the south make it ideal for photographs of 'picture-postcard' sunsets. However, the Muzhapalingau is being promoted as a 'drive-on' beach by the tourist authorities, and so it can get very crowded during holidays.
Continue on National Highway 17 for about 3km (2 miles) to Illukunnu, just off the highway.

2 Illukunnu

German missionary Herman Gundert settled at Illukunnu in 1889 and stayed for about three decades. It was here that he wrote the first Malayalam journal and the first Malayalam–English dictionary. The house is in typical Keralan style but is closed for public viewing.
Return from the house to the highway and drive to Thalasseri.

3 Thalasseri

Thalasseri, or Tellichery, was one of the most important British military bases in Malabar, and it was the site of their first factory in Malabar. The British obtained permission from the Raja of Chirakal to build the fort at Thalasseri in order to protect their interests in spices along the coast and in the hill plantations.

Muslim fishermen at Muzhapalingau Beach

The fort was built in 1708 and successfully withstood the struggle between the British and the Mysorian sultans. Entered by an impressive gate flanked by comical images of guards, the fort has high walls and an abandoned lighthouse, and there are many tales of the secret underground tunnels leading from the fort. Behind it are other colonial buildings, including two churches and a school. The cemetery contains the grave of Edward Brennan, who was the founder of Brennan College, a highly respected institution.

Thalasseri also has old Moplah houses of the Muslim merchant families. Their mosque is in traditional Malabari style, and local accounts say it dates to the 16th century. Thalasseri is also known for its gymnastics school, run by the national sports authority, and for its kalari centre, which instructs students in the traditional martial arts of Kerala. *It is a 23-km (14-mile) drive from Thalasseri back to Kannur.*

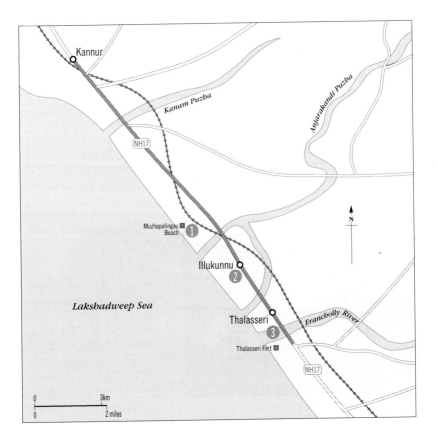

Kasaragode

The name of the northernmost district of Kerala derives its name from the Sanskrit for 'land of lakes'. Ruled by the Nayakas, Kasaragode town fell to Tipu Sultan and came under British rule after the Mysore Wars. It now has a large Muslim population and is known for its mosques, but also has many interesting temples and lovely beaches, so it is being developed into a tourist centre.

Kasaragode is 344km (215 miles) from Cochin, 156km (98 miles) from Kozhikode and 560km (350 miles) from Thiruvananthapuram, with good train connections.

The Anantha Padmanabha Temple, where Puranic murals have been recently restored

Mosques
With a large Muslim population, the town has many mosques, including the beautiful Malik Deenar Jumma Masjid, built in Keralan style. This mosque is believed to be the burial site of Malik Ibn Dinar.

KASARAGODE ENVIRONS
Anantha Padmanabha Temple
This temple is believed to date from the 9th century, although the present structure is more recent, and it is venerated as the original abode of Padmanabhaswamy, the deity of Thiruvananthapuram. Set in a small lake, the temple has a bridge connecting the *gopuram*, or gatehouse, and the sanctuary. The principal deity, Vishnu, is shown sitting on the serpent Anantha, and not reclining as in the more famous Padmanabhaswamy Temple at

The Malik Deenar Jumma Masjid (mosque), said to be the burial site of Malik Ibn Dinar

Thiruvananthapuram. The murals depicting Puranic themes have been recently restored.
The temple is east of Kasaragode town.

Bekal

Bekal is famous for its fort, which offers superb views of the sea. Originally said to be part of the Kadamba kingdom, Bekal passed on to the Vijayanagara dynasty and the Kolatri Rajas. The fort was probably built in the 17th century when the Nayakas took Bekal after the decline of Vijayanagara. Tipu Sultan took Bekal and the British occupied the fort after they defeated the sultan. The walls of the fort are still intact, and a tunnel leads from the interior of the fort directly to the sea.

Dedicated to Hanuman, Anjaneya Temple is built against the fort walls, while south of the fort is Bekal Beach. 6km (3.75 miles) from the fort is another good beach, at Kappil.
The fort is open from 9am–5.50pm. Nominal admission fee and a video camera charge.

Chandgiri Fort

This is one of a string of fortresses built along the coast by the Nayakas in the 17th century. Though largely neglected, Chandgiri Fort is worth visiting for its good sea views.

Kottancherry

Kottancherry is a pleasant place for walks in the Western Ghats.

Nileshwar

Nileshwar is known for its government-approved yoga institute.

Nileshwar is south of Kasaragode past Bekal towards Kannur. For information about yoga courses contact the institute at 0499-280490.

PUPPETRY IN KERALA

Yakshagana Bombeyatta is a form of puppetry that now, sadly, has few practitioners, although some can still be seen in Kasaragode. It is based on the Yakshagana folk theatre of Karnataka, and uses song and elaborately costumed puppets to relate tales from the Hindu epics. String puppets and rod puppets are used, and their costumes and movements enact the role of the character in the story. Sri Gopalakrishna Yakshagana Bombeyatta Sanga at Kasaragode is an organisation promoting and performing this folk art.

Puppetry also survives as a performing art form in Palakad district, and the village of Partithupuli is home to the Adi Pandaram puppeteers who came to Kerala from Andhra Pradesh. Despite its origins in Telugu, the language of Andhra Pradesh, this form of glove puppetry is influenced by Pavakathali, the Kathakali dance drama. Pavakathali employs painted puppets decorated with peacock feathers to portray scenes from the *Mahabharata* and other epics.

Tolpava Koothu, literally 'leather puppet play', enacts tales from the Ramayana by projecting shadows of leather puppets onto a white background. This is a ritualised folk art performed on a stage facing the deity, Kali, and 100 or so puppets can be used in a single performance.

Wayanad District

Wayanad is one of the most forested districts of Kerala, and it has a high tribal population. The district is also known for its waterfalls and wildlife. The name, Wayanad, is believed to be a shortened version of the word Valnadu, meaning 'land of paddy', and the local economy thrives on rice fields, tea, coffee and spice plantations.

The headquarters of Wayanad District is Kalpetta, 251km (157 miles) from Cochin, 63km (39 miles) from Kozhikode and 467km (292 miles) from Thiruvananthapuram.

A tribal woman from Paniyar, Wayanad

Edakkal

The Edakkal Caves comprise Kerala's most famous prehistoric site, featuring prehistoric petroglyphs sculpted into the rocks. The drawings are formed by geometric lines and are generally dated to about 10,000 BC. Some scripts are said to be dated from the 3rd century BC. There are also good views of the surrounding hills.

Heritage Museum

This museum exhibits archaeological finds from the district, mainly 14th- to 16th-century sculptures of deities, as well as tribal artefacts such as local jewellery, weapons and fish traps, and agricultural implements.

Manantwadi

Manantwadi has a 19th-century church that serves the Christian converts among the local tribal population, especially the Kuruchiyas. The churchyard has some old tombstones.
Manantwadi is north of Kalpetta.

Plantations

Wayanad has a number of tea, coffee and spice plantations. The district is also one of the highest producers of arecanuts (beetlenuts). The Patchilakkad Arecanut Factory usually welcomes visitors to see the various processes involved in getting the arecanut ready for market.
Hotels and resorts at Vythri and Kalpetta arrange plantation visits.

Pookote

Pookote has a lake that has been developed for recreational tourism with boating facilities. Opposite the lake is Narayana Guru Ashram.

Ancient tombstones in the Manantwadi churchyard

Sultan's Bathery

This town is named after Tipu Sultan, but there are few signs of the sultan's fort which the British destroyed. There is a Jain temple in the town which probably dates from the 12th or 13th century, and which has carved ceilings. *Regular buses from Mysore, Kalpetta and Kozhikode. Sultan's Bathery has hotels and restaurants.*

Thirunelly

Thirunelly has an important Vishnu Temple, sometimes called 'the Kashi of Kerala'. Devotees bathe in a mountain stream called Papanasini, which they believe brings visitors eternal bliss. *North of Kalpetta via Manantwadi.*

Wildlife reserves

Wayanad Wildlife Sanctuary forms part of the Nilgiri Biosphere Reserve. Access is from Tholpetty near Manantwadi in the north, or from Muthunga near Sultan's Bathery in the south. Across the border in Karnataka, Nagarhole or Rajiv Gandhi National Park can be accessed from Karapur near Manantwadi and Bandipur National Park by continuing on the road past the Muthunga entrance. You are likely to see elephants, sambar, spotted and barking deer, gaur or Indian bison, wild boar, hanuman langur and bonnet macaque. Fortunate visitors could spot sloth bear, but tiger, panther and dhole (wild dog) sightings are rare. Mastigudi in Nagarhole is a good place to see large herds of elephant during the dry months. These forests are also rich in birdlife, including grey jungle fowl, red spurfowl, Malabar pied hornbill, hill mynah, crested serpent eagle, hawk eagle, and many other colourful species. Wetland birds can be seen along the Kabini River.

A permit for the Wayanad sanctuaries can be obtained from Muthunga or Tholpetty. Admission, vehicle entry, guide and camera charges to be paid to the local forest officer. There are usually jeeps standing near the forest department offices for hire to visit the sanctuary.

12th century Jain temple at Sultan's Bathery

Getting Away from It All

It is easy to escape the crowded cities, towns and tourist centres of Kerala by taking an Ayurvedic programme, a houseboat cruise or a tour of wildlife reserves.

Excursion boat, Periyar

AYURVEDIC RESORTS

A number of resort companies and hoteliers have developed health resorts to make the most of the popularity of Ayurvedic massages (*see pp88–9*). The government has set guidelines for Ayurvedic resorts, with 'Green Leaf' and 'Olive Leaf' classifications for those which meet the various standards, such as qualified physicians, separate rooms and therapists for men and women, washrooms and equipment. Ayurvedic centres outside resorts have also received government approval based on the guidelines.

HOUSEBOATS

Few visitors return from Kerala without taking a boat trip on the backwaters (*see pp94–5*). One of the means of travelling the backwaters is by chartered houseboat, which allows more flexibility to plan an itinerary than the tour boats and passenger ferries. The houseboats have been created using the basic design of traditional cargo boats, called *kettuvallams*, and have bedrooms, modern baths, living areas and patios. The length of the boat usually determines the number of bedrooms. Most houseboats have a kitchenette or a separate kitchen in a smaller boat which is towed behind, and most boats have overhead water tanks and solar-powered lighting. The chartered

houseboat comes with a crew of between three and five, including a cook and help. Some of the houseboats have been mechanised for long-distance travel, but many are manually oared. The cruising is generally done during the day, and the boat is then securely anchored at night.

Although the government has laid down guidelines for quality, comfort, construction, environment-friendliness, cleanliness and so on, it is a good idea to find out about the facilities on board before chartering the houseboat. The boats are classified into 'gold star' and 'silver star', according to the services offered. With a wide range of waterways to choose from, travellers can select their own route, and a typical houseboat cruise can include villages, coir factories, plantations, and places of interest such as temples and ashrams.

The price is based on the route, the facilities and services, the duration of the cruise, the size of the houseboat, the number of rooms, and the meals. Trips usually start at Alappuzha, Kollam, Kottayam or Kumarakom, but other stretches, such as the southern backwaters near Thiruvananthapuram and the northern backwaters near Kozhikode and Bekal, are also being promoted for cruising.

Government tourist offices and tour operators can be contacted to book a

*houseboat. Hotels and resorts of Kollam,
Alappuzha and Kottayam District usually
have their own houseboats or can arrange
one according to your requirements.*

SANCTUARIES AND NATIONAL PARKS OF KERALA
Aralam Wildlife Sanctuary

This sanctuary, near Kannur, is home to
elephant, mouse deer and sambar,
besides a range of birds, but has not
been developed for visitors.
*This sanctuary has limited facilities for
tourists. Contact the Aralam Wildlife
Division, Irrity, Kannur District.
Tel: 0497-670673 for more information.*

Chinnar

Set along the Kerala–Tamil Nadu border,
the Chinnar sanctuary comprises mainly
deciduous forests and scrub flora, and is
well known for its grizzled giant squirrel,
which is an endangered species. Other
wildlife, including elephant, gaur and
tiger, can sometimes be spotted, and lots
of langur, macaque and peafowl can be
seen. This is also a very good birding area.
Permission to stay at the forest rest houses
is hard to obtain, and most visitors make
the trip from Munnar or stay in simple
highway hotels near Marayoor.
See p123 for more information.

Eravikulam National Park

The highlight of the 97sq km (61 sq mile)
Eravikulam National Park is the Nilgiri
tahr, best seen in the Rajmalai range.
There is also a variety of birds typical of
the Nilgiri habitat, and the park has
elephant, tiger, leopard, Nilgiri langur,
lion-tailed macaque and giant squirrel,
but special permissions are needed to visit

the interiors of the sanctuary. Munnar,
16km (10 miles) away, has a wide range of
hotels, resorts and guest houses offering
good accommodation.
*See p122 for more information on
Rajmalai, an easily accessible area to
view the Nilgiri tahr.*

Idukki Sanctuary

This sanctuary is home to elephant, gaur
bison, sloth bear, wild boar, deer and
dhole wild dog. The nearest place to stay
is Kottayam, 20km (12.5 miles) away.

Kumarakom Bird Sanctuary

Set along the Vembanad Lake, this bird
sanctuary is home to darters,
cormorants, herons and egrets, and
attracts migratory birds in winter.
*Resorts at Kumarakom arrange boating
and houseboats to tour the sanctuary.*

Neyyar Sanctuary

The 128-sq km (80-sq mile) Neyyar
sanctuary has a 9-sq km (5.5-sq mile)
reservoir offering boat safaris. The
sanctuary has elephants, tigers, bear,
gaur, deer, wild boar, lion-tailed macaque
and Nilgiri langur. The landscape is
breathtakingly beautiful, and the boat ride
through narrow channels, past islands and
along woodlands is exciting. The higher
ranges are covered by grassland inhabited
by tahr and other herbivores, but it can be
difficult to obtain permission for trekking.
There is a lion safari park, as well as a
crocodile park. Basic accommodation
and meals are available locally, but it is
best to make the trip from Trivandrum
32km (20 miles) away.
*Regular buses to Neyyar from
Thiruvananthapuram. Kerala Tourism*

Development Corporation runs a hotel and cafeteria near the dam. Boats can be hired for a tour of the lake.

Parambikulam

This 285-sq km (178-sq mile) sanctuary is one of the finest places to view gaur (Indian bison) in southern India. The checklist includes tiger, panther, wild boar, elephant, langur, macaques and tahr in the forest, and crocodiles and otters at the reservoirs, but accommodation can be a problem with only spartan forest rest houses near the sanctuary. Most visitors make a trip from Coimbatore or Pallakad, both more than 100km (62.5 miles) away.
For more information contact the Wildlife Warden/Deputy Forest Officer of Parambikulam Division (tel: 0425-2367233) or the Wildlife Warden of Annamalai at Pollachi (tel: 04259-225356).

Peechi-Vazhani Sanctuary

Peechi-Vazhani Sanctuary's 125sq km (178sq mile) of moist deciduous teak and rosewood forests is a good place to watch 60 species of birds including grey jungle fowl, peafowl, forest species and waterfowl. The mammal checklist includes elephant, tiger, panther, various species of deer, and gaur (Indian bison). The impressive floral diversity includes 50 species of orchids and medicinal plants. The Peechi and Vazhani dams, from which the sanctuary gets its name, offer boating facilities.
Buses run to Peechi Dam from Thrissur. Permits from the Wildlife Warden at Thrissur, about 20 km (12.4 miles) from the sanctuary. Tel: 2782017.

Peppara Wildlife Sanctuary

This 53-sq km (33-sq mile) sanctuary, near Trivandrum, has a fine reputation as a spot for birdwatching. It is also inhabited by elephant, sambar, leopard and macaque. Check opening hours before visiting, as these can be very erratic.
About 50km (31 miles) from Thiruvananthapuram. Contact the District Forest Office at Thiruvananthapuram. Tel: 0471-2325385.

Periyar National Park

Periyar is one of the leading tiger reserves of India, but few visitors get to see a tiger during their visit to the park. Spanning 777sq km (486sq miles), the mixed forest of deciduous, semi-evergreen and evergreen flora is set around a 55-sq km (34-sq mile) reservoir that is the epicentre for wildlife viewing by boat. The wildlife here includes tiger, sloth bear, wild dog, elephant, sambar, barking deer, mouse deer, wild boar, otter, porcupine, civet, common and Nilgiri langurs, lion-tailed and bonnet macaque, giant and flying squirrel, great and grey hornbill, darters, cormorants, mynahs, orioles, racket-tailed and other drongoes, bulbuls, kingfishers and birds of prey. Turtles, snakes and lizards of various species can be seen basking near the lake.
See pp114–115.

Shenduruny Wildlife Sanctuary

The Shenduruny moist deciduous forests span an area of about 100sq km (62.5sq miles). The sanctuary mainly comprises hill tracts centred around the 26-sq km (16-sq mile) Parappar dam. The sanctuary checklist includes elephant, tiger, leopard, gaur, several species of deer, wild boar, lion tailed macaque and langur. The Shenduruny River flows through the forests and on its banks are Mesolithic painted caves. The sanctuary is 66km (41 miles) by road from Kollam town but has very few facilities for tourists.

Contact The Wildlife Warden, Shenduruny Wildlife Sanctuary, Thenmala Dam PO, Thiruvananthapuram. Tel: 2344600.

Silent Valley National Park

This prime rainforest of 90sq km (56sq miles) came into the limelight during the 1984 national campaign to save it from a proposed dam project. The park is well known for its endangered species of monkey, as well as birds and butterflies. The sanctuary is also home to tiger, panther, elephant and tahr. Palakad, 85km (53 miles) away, is the nearest place with good accommodation. Permission to stay in the forest's rest houses can be hard to obtain, because this substantial tract of rainforest is strictly protected.

Contact: Assistant Wildlife Warden, Silent Valley Range, PO Mukkali, District Palakkad. Tel: 0492-2453225.

Thatekkad Sanctuary

This is one of the best bird sanctuaries in Kerala. Located on the banks of a river and interspersed with stretches of water, the forests are excellent for spotting Malabar hornbill, frogmouth, and broad-billed roller, and visitors can expect to see species of oriole, leaf bird, flycatcher, drongo, mynah, woodpecker, sunbird and bee-eater during a three- or four-hour walk in the tall forests. Elephants come down for water in the dry months, and the higher forests harbour many large mammals.

Thatekkad is 15km (9.3 miles) north from the main road connecting Cochin with Munnar.

Wayanad Wildlife Sanctuary

An impressive sanctuary of deciduous and bamboo forests, swamps and grasslands, Wayanad borders Nagarhole and Bandipur Tiger Reserve in Karnataka. The sanctuary is a fine place to see elephant and gaur, as well as spotted deer, sambar, barking deer, wild boar, langur and macaque. Sloth bear, tiger and panther are also present in this area, and a good variety of birds, including peafowl and grey jungle fowl, can be seen. The two entrances, Tholpetty and Muthunga, can be visited from Kalpetta, the district headquarters. *See p138.*

EXCURSIONS

A tour of Kerala can also be combined with visits to places in neighbouring states. Some examples are as follows:

Kanyakumari and Padmanabhapuram

These two places in Tamil Nadu form an easy day excursion from Thiruvananthapuram or Kovalam (*see pp86–7*).

Madikeri (Karnataka)

Madikeri is the capital of Kodagu District, or the region of Coorg, and can be visited for a night or more from Kannur. The town is the commercial centre of coffee and other plantations, and among its many attractions are the Omkareshwara Temple, Raja's Seat with views of the hills, and the nearby Abby Falls.

Shopping

Shopping in India can be an exciting experience. Besides their own products, the markets at the tourist centres of Goa and Kerala are inundated with handicrafts from other parts of India. This means that in Goa, which is not particularly well-known for handicrafts, you can find textiles and handiwork from Kashmir, Tibet, Nepal, Gujarat, Rajasthan and South India. The range of textiles is vast, from reasonably priced block-printed fabrics and tie-dye from Rajasthan and Gujarat, to high-priced silk saris from Kanchipuram, Orissa, Andhra and Varanasi. However, Goa and Kerala are perhaps best known for their spices and cashew nuts.

Shopping in the hills near Idduki

How to shop

At established shops, prices are generally fixed and there is no real room for bargaining, although some shops will give you a deal for large purchases. It may be a good idea to check the prices at different shops before buying, as the discounts may vary. Shops usually announce 'clearance sales', 'discount sales', 'off-season sales' and 'festival discounts' in the newspapers or declare them on banners.

At street-side markets and at flea markets the prices are usually marked up and there is considerable room for bargaining. In tourist centres, vendors generally hike the price up and you might do well by halving the asking price and then reaching an agreement. Walk away slowly in order to gauge the response of the vendor, and you will usually be called back for further negotiation. Shop owners and sales people can be very persuasive, so it is important to be firm and not be swayed.

What to buy

Goa has excellent cashew nuts and locally grown spices, which can be bought at shops in towns such as Panaji, Ponda, Madgaon and Mapusa. Kerala is good for tea, coffee and spices such as cardamom, cinnamon, ginger, pepper and nutmeg.

It is illegal to take genuine antiques out of India, without proper licensing, but you can find good copies in the markets.

Where to buy

Government-owned emporia are generally safe bets for genuine quality at fixed prices, but sometimes private shops also claim to be government emporia. Hotel shopping malls and big shops also guarantee quality, although they may be more expensive.

In Kerala, some factories are also open for visitors to see their processes, such as weaving, coir making or tea production, and it is then possible to buy from the factory outlet.

There is no dearth of markets in India. They are good places to look for fresh fruits, vegetables, meats and fish, and to find bargains.

Old city bazaars are atmospheric and full of colour, and the maze of streets and alleys are lined with vendors, open-air stalls and shops selling a wide range of products for the locals, including utensils, jewellery, clothes and food.

GOA
Art and antiques
Aged Antiquards
Sapana Garden, Chogem Road, Porvorim.
The Attic
Camarcazana, Mapusa. Tel: 22257690.
Saudade
Chogem Road, Sangolda.

Contemporary art galleries
Art Chamber
Art gallery featuring different artists.
115a Gauravaddo, Calangute.
Tel: 2277144 .
Kerkar Art Gallery
Gallery of paintings and sculptures by Dr Subodh Kerkar, housed in Kerkar Art Complex, which holds performances, exhibitions and workshops.
Gauravaddo, Calangute. Tel: 2276017.
www.subodhkerkar.com
Omar's Art Bolcao
Art gallery.
Varca, Salcette. Tel: 2745115.
Panjim Inn & Panjim Pousada
These two heritage hotels have art galleries exhibiting works by different artists.
E-212, 31st Jan Road, Fontainhas, Panjim. Tel: 2226523.

Shireen Mody
Gallery displaying Shireen Mody's acrylic paintings.
33/1 Voegas Vado, Arpora, Bardez.
Tel: 2745115.

Books
There are good bookshops at Mandovi Hotel, Panaji and Bogmalo Beach Resort.
Bookmark
Da Costa Chambers, Madgaon.
Tel: 2711796.
Utopia
Dr A Borkar Road, Panaji.
Varsha
Azad Maidan, Panaji.

Department stores
Saga
Mobor, Cavellossim.

Handicrafts
Carlo Menze Collections
For ceramics, cabinets and Chinese arts.
Rua San Tome, Panaji. Tel: 2422587.
Heirlooms
Selling ceramic and other handicrafts.
Junta House, June 18th Road, Panaji.
Tel: 2224788.
Manthan
Lifestyle store, with antiques, paintings and handicrafts.
1346 Manzil Vaddo, Benaulim.
Nyara
Textiles and handicrafts shop.
Near Miranda House, Loutolim.
Villa Saligao
This cottage industry emporium sells a wide variety of handicrafts, including jewellery, carpets and textiles.
H295 Piqueno Morod, Chogem Road, Saligao. Tel: 2409756.

Garments and boutiques

Archana
Indian designer dresses.
Padmavati Towers, 18th June Road, Panaji.

Bandhej
Indian contemporary and traditional clothes.
Navalkar Trade Centre, opp. Azad Maidan, Panaji.

Carey Franklin
Garments, T-shirts and accessories.
Church Square, Panaji.

Caro's
Clothes shop.
Near Municipality Garment, Madgaon.
Tel: 2705659.

Exact
Ladies' clothes shop.
GS/14 Padmavati Towers, 18th June Road, Panaji.

J & B
Boutique.
Behind Grace Church, Madgaon.

Julies Darwin
Leather boutique.
Souza Enclave, Madgaon.

Madame Butterfly
Designer dresses and accessories.
Navelkar Trade Centre, MG Road, Azad Maidan, Panaji. Tel: 2222561.

Raymonds
Men's clothes shop.
Blue Pearl Theatre, Madgaon.
Tel: 2711501.

Seniors
Clothes and shoes.
Kundaikar Nagar, Near Hari Mandir, Madgaon.

Sosa's
Boutique.
E-245 Rua Do Oorum, Panaji.
Tel: 2228062.

Svelte
Boutique.
Midland Aprs, Miguel Loyola Furtado Road, Madgaon.

Velho e Filhos
Branded garments.
Opp. Municipal Garden, Panaji.
Tel: 2425338.

Wendell Rodericks
Boutique and showroom.
B-5 Suryadarshan Colony, Altinho, Panaji.

Gifts and stationery

Paperworks
F-2 Pinto Arcade, Campal, Panaji.

Ritika
Bookshop, boutique, stationery and gifts.
Bogmalo Beach Resort, Bogmalo.

Jewellery

Intergold
9 Mascarenhas Building, MG Road, Panaji.

Verlekar
New Market, Madgaon. Tel: 2736081.

Lifestyle

Camelot
Designer dresses and handicrafts in a converted heritage house.
139 Fondvem, Rbandar. Tel: 2444255.

Sangolda
Attractive lifestyle shop.
E-2 Chogem Road, Sangolda.

Music

Pedro Fernandes
19 Av D Joao Castro, GPO, Panaji.

Rock n Raaga
Rizvi Towers, 18th June Road, Panaji.

Sinari's
18th June Road, Panaji.

Vibes
Anna Felicia, Comba, Madgaon.

Textiles
Caro Corner
New Market, Madgaon.
Co-optex
EDC house, Panaji.

THIRUVANANTHAPURAM
Books
DC
Statue Junction.
Higginbotham's
MG Road.
India Book House
MG Road.
Modern Book Centre
Pulimuddu Junction.
Pai & Co
MG Road.

Handicrafts
Co-optex
Temple Road.
Gift Corner
MG Road.
Handloom House
Near East Fort.
Hastakala
Indian arts and crafts.
Off MG Road.
Kairalai
Government-sponsored emporia.
Tourist facilitation Centre, Museum Road.
Kalanjali
Palace Garden.
Natesan's Antiqarts
Opp. Ayurveda College, MG Road. Tel: 2331594.

Partha's
A range of textiles.
Near East Fort.
SMSM Institute
Government-supported showroom, with a wide range of Keralan handicrafts.
YMCA Road. Tel: 2330298.

COCHIN
Art
Chitram Art Gallery
MG Road, Ernakulam.
Dravidia Art & Performance Gallery
Kalvatty near Fort Kochi.
Galleria Mareecheka
Chittoor Road.
Galleria Synagogue
Mattancherry.

Books
Idiom Books
Synagogue Lane, Jew Town.
DC Books
Opp. Saritha, Banerji Road. Tel: 239128.
Paico
MG Road, Ernakulam Business Centre.

Handicrafts
Kairali
Handicraft emporium.
MG Road. Tel: 2354507.

Jewellery
Allapat Fashion Jewellery
MG Road, Ernakulam. Tel: 2352149.
Alukkas
MG Road.

Textiles
Parthas Textiles
MG Road. Tel: 355699.

Arts and Crafts of Kerala

Patronised by the princely states and temple builders, the artists and artisans of Kerala excelled in painting and sculpture.

Painting

The painting traditions that began in rock-cut temple caves more than 1000 years ago, reached their zenith in the temples of the 16th to the 18th centuries, such as Ettumanoor, the palace of the Rajas of Cochin, and even in the churches of Kerala. Drawing heavily from the style of the Pallava, Hoysala and Vijayanagar School, these murals were distinctive in their use of colour, line and subject matter.

Some people believe that the origins of Keralan mural painting can be traced back to *Kalamezhuttu*, ritual drawings of deities and *mandalas* (geometric patterns), made with coloured powder. Each colour derives from natural sources such as rice flour, turmeric, leaves and burnt husk, and is applied using the thumb and forefinger.

Sculpture

Like painting, woodcarving developed in Kerala with patronage from the landed families and the temple builders. Sandalwood, teakwood and rosewood sculpture, especially those of Hindu deities, can be seen in a number of cities and towns. Toys, lacquered woodwork, Kathakali models and wooden furnishings are sold at emporia and in the markets.

Metalwork

The traditional medium for metal sculpture is a blend of gold, silver,

copper, iron and tin (called *panchaloha*), but bronze sculptures of deities also became popular because of their durability. Bell metal, comprising mainly copper, is commonly used today for metal crafts, such as temple bells, which are said to have a special chime when struck. One of the most famous centres for metalwork is Nadavaramba, near

Irinjalakuda, which manufactures oil lamps and cooking utensils.

Gold jewellery

For the people of Kerala, gold symbolises light, eternity, wealth and purity. Gold jewellery is therefore present at auspicious occasions, particularly births and weddings. In the past, the design of the jewellery often denoted the community to which the wearer belonged, but now patterns are universal and range from the plain to the elaborate. The Nagapadam is a serpent pendant, once popular with Nair women, and generally in the shape of a cobra hood. The Kasumala is a gold coin necklace, usually depicting the Goddess Laxmi, although some kasumalas also portray British royalty. The Tali necklace tied around the neck of a bride has an Om if she is a Hindu and a cross if she is Christian. The Cheruthali necklace is an

ornament of the Namboodiri Brahmin women, and the Oddiyanam waist belt is extremely popular among Tamil Brahmins. The Vanki is a forearm ornament generally used during weddings, whilst gold earrings, especially the bell-like jhimka, are also popular in Kerala. The Mekka Mothiram was a popular ornament of the Christian community in Kerala, and the Mangamala is a necklace with a mango motif. The jasmine-shaped pendant is called a Mullamottu, and the Palaka is a gold ornament set with green glass. The jewellers of Kerala rarely set other stones into gold jewellery, and although contemporary designs are coming into fashion, most of them are still based on traditional patterns. No visitor to Kerala, especially to the central region from Cochin to Kozhikode, can fail to notice the number of hoardings advertising gold jewellery.

Other handicrafts

Kerala is well known for weaving of various kinds, including coir weaving, reed weaving, screw pine mat weaving, and grass mat weaving, as well as embroidery and lace making. Some weaving units have started using jute as a substitute to coir and cane.

Opposite: Painted Hindu deity at a Goan temple
Above: Wood carvings of Hindu deities have been prevalent in Kerala since temples were first built

Entertainment

The Goans are known for their lively music and dance (*see pp12–13*), and you will hear English, Indian and Konkani pop music wherever you go. Entertainment in Kerala generally revolves around traditional performances of dance drama, Carnatic music and martial arts.

Painting of Vasco da Gama meeting the Zamorin

GOA
Art Galleries

Goa is known for its artists, including contemporary painters and sculptors, cartoonists and illustrators. The state has a number of art galleries showing permanent exhibitions; temporary exhibitions are held at Kala Academy.

Bar sign in Vasco da Gama, Goa

Cinema

It is easy to find a cinema almost anywhere in India showing the popular Hindi films churned out by the massive Bombay (Mumbai)-based film industry described as 'Bollywood'. English-language films are also occasionally shown.

With Goa's plans for a huge international film festival in 2005, the cinema halls are expected to improve and new multiplexes are likely to be built in the near future.

Cultural Centres

Kala Academy is Goa's main cultural centre, where performances, from classical to contemporary, are held in an award-winning auditorium. Goan theatre, music, dance and other regional performances are staged at this centre, which also has exhibition galleries and a library. Marathi and Konkani performing arts festivals are also organised at the Academy. *D Bandodkar Marg, Campal, Panaji. Tel: 223288.*

Kerkar Art Complex has regular Indian classical

concerts, dance performances and other cultural programmes.
Gaurawado, Calangute. Tel: 226017.

Nightlife
Many hotels, resorts and restaurants have live bands or employ singers on most nights to entertain diners. Goans love to party and the scene can get lively during festivals, feasts and the Carnival. Goa is known for its travellers' parties at the beaches, but these can get out of hand and are sometimes raided by the authorities if they suspect that drugs are being used.

Goa also has bars, discos and casinos, mostly at hotels and resorts. Evening cruises with on-board cafeteria and bar, and short performances of local music and dance, continue to be popular, but they can be a little disappointing.

A classical Keralan dance performance

Keralan photographer in his studio

Thiruvananthapuram is the site for an International Film Festival, and the city has many cinemas showing Indian films, as well as some English-language films.

Kallaripayattu

It is possible to see students learning the martial art of Kalaripayattu (*see pp80–81*) or masters practising at gymnasiums called kalaris in almost every city or town of Kerala. Demonstrations are often available if advance notice is given. You can also make appointments for Ayurvedic treatments, and short-term courses are run at some kalaris.

CVN Kalari Sangham, *East Fort, Nr Sri Padmanabhaswamy Temple, Thiruvananthapuram. Tel: 2474182.*

Anjuna Kalari Centre, *Ernakulam. Tel: 365440.*

ENS Kalari Centre, *Nettoor, Kochi.*

CVN Kalari, *P.O. Edakkad, Calicut. Tel: 0495-2391808.*

KERALA
Art galleries

The art galleries in the museum complex at Thiruvananthapuram hold regular exhibitions of contemporary artists. Cochin has exhibitions and performances at Galleria Synagogue, Dravidia Art & Performance Gallery, Art Café and Kashi.

Cinema

South India has a thriving film industry, with Malayalam films having been made for more than 75 years.

Kathakali

One of the four main classical styles of India, the dance drama follows certain norms but is dynamic and has accepted various changes over the years, such as replacing the mask with stiff make-up (*see pp112–13*). In order to make the dance drama form more popular, shorter versions have been created for tourists.

The ritualised dance drama form of Kathakali is performed at the temple theatres of Kerala, but these are rarely open for non-Hindus. A good alternative, however, is to see a performance at a cultural centre.

Cochin Cultural Centre, *Souhardham, Manikath Road, Kochi. Tel: 0484-2367866.*

Kerala Kathakali Centre, *Cochin Aquatic Club, River Road, Fort Kochi.*

See India Foundation, *Kalathiparambil Lane, Ernakulam. Tel: 0484-2368471.*

Art Kerala, *Kannanthodathu Lane, Valajambalam, Ernakulam. Tel: 0484-2366231.*

Hotels at Thiruvananthapuram, Kovalam and Cochin also stage Kathakali shows on a regular basis: ask at the tourist offices for information.

Music

Kerala is known for its Carnatic music, and you should be able to find out about performances in all the major cities. Ghazals and other Hindustani music is popular in Kozhikode.

Kathakali performances can be seen at cultural centres as well as temple theatres

Children

India is a family-oriented society where children are welcomed, and this warmth is extended to those travelling with them. Children are very popular in India and most Indians will bend over backwards to help you. Children are welcomed in most hotels and restaurants, religious places and at the various tourist sites and monuments. However, travelling with children in India does involve a few hazards of which you need to be aware.

Goan girl

ACCOMMODATION

It makes sense to find a good hotel for your base while in India. Most chefs will prepare food to your requirements and there is usually a mini-bar with bottled water and snacks. Hotels will happily supply an extra bed or a family room at a supplement, although children below the age of ten are not usually charged for occupying a room. Some hotels and resorts are geared up for children, with play areas, toddlers' pools, indoor games, movies, competitions and special menus, but it is best to find out about the facilities when you book. Some hotels may be able to arrange babysitters.

FOOD

It may be a good idea to carry baby food with you, particularly if your child has particular favourites which may not be available. At hotels, resorts and restaurants there is generally a large menu, with good options for children. Eggs, biscuits, bread, butter, cheese, chocolate, bottled drinks, ice cream, packaged and canned foods are generally available everywhere.

Syrian Orthodox children carry banners during a festival

HEALTH

Those travelling with babies and children need to be careful. Besides all the necessary vaccinations (see p185), children should also be protected against diphtheria, whooping cough, mumps, measles and Hepatitis B.

Local people love children and will offer them sweets and fruits, so it is important to be vigilant about this when travelling with children.

ON THE ROAD

Long journeys with children in India can be difficult, so it's best to base yourself in just one or two places. If you are renting a car, buying a child's car seat is a good idea. Bathrooms are rarely clean; taking a portable toilet seat with you may help. There are grocery stores on the roadside, and snacks are available on board the trains, but it's best to pack some snacks for your journey. Biscuits, chocolates and soft drinks are easily available.

Your children may be disturbed by the attention lavished on them by Indians, so you need to be prepared for this.

PACKING

Nappies and toiletries are available in Indian cities, but emergency supplies are recommended. Also, make sure you bring any medicines which you may need, as well as a first-aid kit. It is a good idea to pack some toys and books to keep children amused.

There are plenty of shops to buy provisions for children

Keralan children on Kappad Beach

THINGS TO DO

India does not have any of the large amusement parks that children look forward to visiting. However, children will probably enjoy the general liveliness of India, where getting around in auto-rickshaws, trains, ferries and chartered boats can be fun. Rides on elephants, camels, ponies and boats are also great favourites.

Beaches

Goa's coastline is lined with excellent beaches and you are really spoilt for choice. The northern beaches are usually more popular and crowded, with beach restaurants and shacks, while the southern beaches are mainly visited by those staying at the hotels and upmarket beach resorts that overlook them. The beaches near Panaji, such as Dona Paula and Miramar, are popular locally. Most beach resorts cater for children and even organise activities such as sandcastle competitions.

In Kerala, Kovalam is a popular beach destination, while other beaches, including Marari near Alappuzha, have recently been developed. Most cities and towns along the coast, such as Kasaragode, Bekal, Kannur, Thalasseri, Kozhikode, Thrissur, Cochin, Alappuzha, Kollam and Thiruvananthapuram, have good beaches that are popular for day trips. Before entering the water, check that it is safe to swim or paddle there; some beaches have lifeguards who will show you the safest areas.

Backwaters

Cruising the backwaters can be great fun

for children, and speedboats can also be hired for short journeys.

Boat Trips
A number of boat trips are on offer at Goa and Kerala, including dolphin viewing and sunset cruises.

In town
All cities and towns have parks and gardens, with paths for a pleasant stroll and with areas for children to play.

Lakes
The Mayem Lake at Goa, and many lakes of Kerala, have been developed as 'picnic spots', with boating and other recreational facilities. Some waterfalls are also promoted as 'picnic spots'.

Waiting at a boat stop on the backwaters

Shopping
The Indian bazaars and handicraft emporia can be fun for children. Locally made dolls dressed in the attires of different states of India, Kerala's papier mâché Kathakali masks, handcrafted wooden toys and miniature boats are favourites. However, make sure that the toys you buy are safe for children.

Wildlife reserves
Seeing big animals is exciting for children. Periyar is well developed for travellers, with a wide choice of places to stay and eat, including the upmarket resorts of Kumily and Thekkadi. The two-hour launch cruises offer scenic views of the forests, and large mammals including elephants can usually be spotted. Wayanad Wildlife Sanctuary also offers good opportunities for wildlife sightings, and there are hotels and resorts at Vythri, Kalpetta and Sultan's Bathery, all of which can arrange high-clearance vehicles and the necessary permits for a visit. Boat rides on the River Kabini can also be arranged by these hotels, or at Nagarhole National Park across in Karnataka.

In Goa, Molem is the centre of wildlife-viewing activities. There are a few hotels and camps at Molem, and also at nearby Tambdi Surla, which can arrange visits to the Bhagwan Mahavir Wildlife Sanctuary. Indian bison and deer are generally seen during short drives. Bondla is more popular as a zoo than as a wildlife sanctuary, unless you visit early in the morning when deer herds are active.

Sport and Leisure

Although sports are not generally associated with India, except, of course, for Himalayan mountaineering, they are nevertheless a popular form of entertainment. All kinds are on offer, from spectator sports to those especially developed for tourism, such as water sports and adventure activities.

Indian tourists enjoy the backwaters

Large hotels and resorts have sports facilities including swimming pools, and many smaller ones have indoor games facilities such as pool tables. The clubs are the best places for sports and leisure, but entry is usually restricted to members. Some clubs have reciprocal arrangements with those elsewhere, whilst some offer temporary membership, and hotels may be able to arrange admission to a club nearby.

Some clubs also have residential rooms, which can be an alternative to staying at hotels, but you may need to be introduced by a member. You could also ask about government-run sports facilities that are open to the general public.

SPORTS FACILITIES
Adventure and water sports

Water-skiing, jet skiing, surfing, yachting, parasailing and other water sports are on offer at many of Goa's beaches, but it is important to inspect the equipment or ask about safety standards, as this is still a fledgling industry. Some resorts also offer these facilities for their guests, and speedboats are becoming popular in both Goa and Kerala.

Kerala promotes adventure sports such as rock-climbing, trekking and hang gliding in the Western Ghats. Most of these trips operate around Munnar, but operators also arrange treks in the Western Ghats near

Boats are prepared for water sport activity

Fishing huts and nets pepper the beach at Kovalam

may be a good idea to bring your own equipment. The prized fish of the Kerala backwaters is *karimean*.

The streams and lakes of the Western Ghats offer good fishing. The High Ranges Anglers Association at Munnar is helpful in giving information and obtaining licences. For more serious fishing, you can pit your might against the mahseer, India's most prized catch, on the River Cauvery in Karnataka. The Anglers Association at Kodagu District, adjoining the Kannur District of Kerala (*see p128*), can assist with information about permits for catch-and-release angling of mahseer on the river. Resort and travel companies, including Jungle Lodges and Resorts at Bangalore, run angling camps along the River Cauvery at spots known for their sport fish.

Private operators in Goa take travellers on boat trips where they can see locals catching deep-sea fish, including shark, and the state government has recently imposed improved regulations and guidelines for safety standards on these boats.

Thiruvananthapuram and in the northern districts of Kerala, such as Kasaragode. The tribal-guided treks in Periyar Tiger Reserve are significant eco-development projects.

For rafting, Dandeli National Park in Karnataka is easily accessible from Goa. The rafting activities on offer range from scenic floats through the forests, which are good for birdwatching and occasional wildlife sightings, to strenuous white-water rafting at the falls. There are resorts and camps near the entrance to the national park.

Angling

Some hotels and resorts have their own ponds, private lakes or backwater inlets where they allow fishing on catch-and-release or you-catch-we-cook basis. Most of them have fishing rods, but it

Basketball

Basketball is a popular game, mainly at school and college level in Goa and

Tourists cycle along Benaulim Beach

Kerala, and both states have basketball associations.

Billiards and snooker

Billiards and snooker are popular in India. Most clubs have a billiards room and some hotels have pool tables.

Cricket

Cricket is the most popular sport in India. Crowds gather in hotels and public places to watch international fixtures on TV, especially if the Indian team is playing. Both Goa and Kerala have state-level cricket associations, and you can observe cricket practice at stadiums and in campuses, as well as informal games played on open ground, and children playing with a bat and ball even in narrow streets. You may even be invited by locals to join a friendly game. At competitive level, cricket is a serious business, and Indian clubs invite foreign teams to play or tour other countries.

Cycling

Goa and Kerala offer a variety of terrain for bicycle touring. Indian bicycles are good for short distances and local sightseeing, but they are not very comfortable for serious touring on hilly roads or rocky paths. You can either join a group tour with everything taken care of by the operator, or bring your own bicycle, preferably a mountain bike. If you bring a bicycle, carry more spares than you think will be needed, including oil and a pump.

Indian cycles can be hired at most cities, towns and villages at very nominal prices. Imported cycles are available only at very popular tourist destinations of Goa and Kerala.

Football

Football is a popular sport in Goa and Kerala. Both states have football clubs that excel in national tournaments, and they usually also have members in the national team. In winter, Goan villages play league games, with sponsored teams such as Salgaokar, Dempo, Sesa Goa and Churchill Brothers. The Nehru Stadium in Madgaon is one of the largest football centres on India's west coast, seating about 34,000, and there is also a football stadium at Panaji. Details of matches are published in the newspapers. Foreign players, especially those from African countries, also take part in Goa's football season.

With the advent of international TV channels in India, soccer is widely followed in the country, and most locals will discuss the last World Cup if they know you have any interest in the game. Brazilian football stars have a large fan following in Goa.

Golf

Kerala has some seven- to nine-hole golf courses, but admission is usually reserved for club members and their guests. The Trivandrum Golf Club's clubhouse was established about a century ago by the Maharaja of Travancore. Munnar has golf courses for the plantation staff and management, and local hotels may be able to help you find a local member who can introduce you as a guest. Bangalore and Kodagu District (*see p143*) in Karnataka, and Ooty in Tamil Nadu, have golf courses but similar restrictions may apply. You can also find out about any local tournaments that allow foreigners to participate.

The Trivandrum Golf Club, Kowdiar, Thiruvananthapuram. Tel: 2435834.
High Range Club, Munnar. Tel: 2530253.

A football field near Reis Magos

Cochin Golf Club, Bolgatty Island.
Tel: 2369908.

Scuba diving

Goa has diving schools, certified by the Professional Association of Diving Instructors, which operate courses and diving trips. The dives near the jetties are shallow, about eight metres, with variable visibility. Some of the sites are off islands, reached after a 15- to 30-minute boat ride. The schools list dive sites for beginners, in sheltered coves and near jetties, but those with strong currents are only suitable for experienced divers. A variety of fish can be seen, as well as crustaceans, morays, hard corals and sea fans, and some of the dive sites include wrecks that are colonised by marine wildlife. Diving trips are also operated to Devbagh Island and other sites in Karnataka near the Goan border.

A number of dive operators run trips at the Lakshadweep Islands, accessible from Cochin by air or ship. Lakshadweep is a union territory, comprising both inhabited and uninhabited islands.
Barracuda Diving India, Goa Marriot Resort, Miramar. Tel: 2437001.
Goa Diving, Chapel Bhat, Chicalim. Tel: 2555117.
Bangaram Island Resort, Lakshadweep (Casino Group, Cochin. Tel: 0484-668221).
The Society for Promotion of Recreational Tourism and Sports in Lakshadweep, Willingdon Island, Kochi.
Tel: 0484-668387.
Lacadives. Tel: 022-56627381/82.

Swimming pools

Almost all resorts and most of the big hotels in Goa and Kerala have a swimming pool. By regulation, swimming pools at Indian hotels and resorts are shallow and prohibit diving. They have separate changing rooms, with showers, for men and women. Towels are provided and many hotels have smaller pools for children, as well as Jacuzzis next to the main pool. Some hotel pools permit non-residents, for an admission charge.

Swimming pools at clubs and sports complexes usually follow international competitive standards regarding size and depth, and many have diving boards.

Tennis, badminton and squash

Most of the bigger resorts and hotels, and almost all clubs, have facilities for these popular games.

ATTENTION

● Nudity on beaches and public places is forbidden and punishable under the law.

● Do not swim in unknown waters and during low tides.
For assistance contact lifeguard / Tourist Police on duty.

● Indulgence in drug offences are punishable under the law with a penalty of ten years rigorous imprisonment and a fine of Rs. 1,00,000/-.

Be mindful of potential hazards in the water

Tourists play volleyball on a Goan beach

Volleyball

Volleyball is popular at school and
college level and you will see volleyball
courts at many villages. Some of the
beaches also have volleyball courts for
visitors.

HEALTH CLUBS AND SPAS
Health clubs

Many hotels and resorts have health
clubs with a gym, sauna and steambath.
Use of the gym is usually free for hotel
residents. Most health clubs are
managed by a team of supervisors
responsible for maintaining the
equipment and assisting guests. A few
hotels and resorts also have daily
aerobics sessions and weight-training
instructors. The health clubs generally
have separate sections for men and
women, but some may also have
different timings.

Long-staying visitors to Goa or
the cities of Kerala can also become
members of health clubs with qualified
instructors. Inspect the equipment and
hygiene standards before joining a
programme.

Strolling around rural India is a feast for the senses

Massages
Masseurs peddle their services at many of the beaches, and hotel health clubs may also have a massage room. Ayurvedic massage centres have opened at some of the tourist centres, with strict guidelines laid down by the respective state governments.

Yoga and meditation
With the increasing international interest in these ancient Asian disciplines for physical and spiritual well-being, several hotels and resorts have made yoga, meditation and Ayurvedic therapies available to their guests. Both short- and long-term courses are offered, and at some upmarket resorts there are daily sessions for beginners at fixed hours.

For more serious yoga students, the beginner and advanced courses at ashrams and government-approved institutions may be preferable. Neyyar near Thiruvananthapuram, and Nileshwar near Kasaragode, are among the most renowned places for yoga instruction.
See Neyyar under Thiruvananthapuram and Nileshwar on p137.

Spas
Besides Ayurvedic massage and therapy, a number of upmarket resorts in Goa have started offering Southeast Asian aromatherapy, Thai and Balinese massage, Swedish massage, hydrotherapy and other spa treatments. Bangalore in Karnataka has spas that offer a variety of treatments 'under one roof'.

WALKING

Goa and Kerala offer plenty of variety for those who love walking. There are narrow roads through the old quarters of cities and towns, village paths that offer a glimpse of rural India, coastal roads through palm groves, winding roads and paths in the hills and in plantation areas, and strenuous treks in the Western Ghats.

BIRDWATCHING

Birdwatching in Goa and Kerala is particularly rewarding. Your hotel should be able to refer you to specialist tour operators or guides that take birdwatching trips or guided nature walks. Visitors to Goa will return with a healthy checklist of birds seen – and even more heard, because spotting is difficult in the Western Ghats – at the various sites in the state.

Besides the wildlife reserves of Goa (*see pp62–3*), birdwatching guides take visitors to the forests of Tambdi Surla, where Malabar hornbill, frogmouth, blue-eared kingfisher, Indian pitta, Malabar trogon, Scops owl, eagle owl and woodpeckers are among the key species. The coastal areas of Morjim are good for shorebirds, whilst Cabo De Rama is renowned for its sea eagles, and Carambolim and Mayem lakes for waterfowl. The best birdwatching in Kerala is generally to be found at the wildlife reserves.

Periyar Wildlife Sanctuary is a serene and scenic area for birdwatching

Food and Drink

Visitors will find a delightful variety of food in Goa and
Kerala. Clustered along the coast, fish and seafood feature
prominently on the menu of the restaurants in both states,
but you will also find lamb, mutton (goat), beef, pork,
chicken and duck, and a variety of fresh vegetables, cooked
in the locally grown spices.

Banana stall, Cochin

Where to eat

Remember that Indian food can be a lot
more spicy on its home ground than at
curry restaurants abroad. Hotels, resorts
and restaurants in the tourist centres are
accustomed to travellers and invariably
prepare food to suit the foreign palate.
The cooks are pretty accommodating
about preparing food according to any
specific dietary or special requests. At
five-star hotels you will find a wide
choice of cuisine, from French and
Italian to Thai, Mughlai and South
Indian, as well as lavish buffets.

Beach cafés and restaurants are
usually temporary shacks or kiosks that
pop up during the holiday season. As
business has boomed for these shacks,
they have drawn cooks from Nepal,
Bengal and North India. The shacks
generally promise fresh seafood. Even
street-side eating places, called *dhabas*,
are relatively safe, as the turnover is
high and the menu is limited to a few
simple items.

Health issues

One of India's greatest health hazards
for visitors is its drinking water.
Drinking straight from a tap, or using
tap water for cleaning teeth, is an open
invitation to water-borne diseases,
as the public water supply is often
contaminated. Bottled water is widely
available, but check the seal properly
and crush the bottle before disposing
of it so that it can't be refilled. At
restaurants, ask for the sealed bottle
to be opened in front of you. If you
are visiting someone's home, ask if
the water is 'purified'. Carry water
sterilisation tablets and a filter just in
case you visit somewhere where bottled
water is not available.

Fruits, vegetables, cold meats and
fish, which have been exposed to flies
or washed in dirty water, as well as
undercooked meats and vegetables, are
risky even in big hotels. Shellfish is not
recommended unless you know that it
is very fresh.

Drinks

Tea, or *chai*, is made in Indian homes
and restaurants by brewing tea leaves,
milk, water and sugar. This is usually a
safe drink to have, and it is often easily
available at street-side kiosks, railway
stations and on trains. *Masala chai*
includes powdered spices such as ginger,
cardamom or cinnamon. If you want
tea in a pot, with milk and sugar served

separately, ask for 'service tea' or 'English tea'.

Coffee is also served white, brewed with milk and sugar unless specified. Espresso and cappuccino are becoming popular at cafés and coffee shops, and South India is famous for its local-style filter coffee.

Another popular beverage in India is *lassi* or *chaas*, which is buttermilk made by churning yoghurt. As this contains water, you need to give the waiter purified water from which to make it. Similarly, make sure that fruit juices are served without water or ice.

Indian makes of whisky, rum, gin and vodka are referred to as 'Indian-made foreign liquors' and are easily available in Goa and Kerala. Foreign brands are available at larger shops and are served at bigger hotels in tourist centres. Some foreign brands of beer are served at the beach shacks. A local Goan drink is *feni*. *Kaju feni* is the fermented juice of the cashew apple, while *coconut feni* or *palm feni* is the fermented sap of the coconut palm. Locals drink it 'on the rocks' or 'neat', but it is an acquired taste. You can try it with soda or in a fruit cocktail.

Breakfast
At hotels, breakfast is usually a lavish buffet, but it can also be a set American, Continental or Indian menu.

If you are eating out at street-side restaurants, the usual breakfast options are *puri* (deep-fried whole wheat rounds) with vegetables, *parathas* (Indian whole wheat bread cooked and usually stuffed with potatoes and other vegetables), *idlis* (rice dumplings), *wadas* (deep-fried savoury doughnuts) or *dosas* (savoury rice pancakes, usually stuffed with potatoes, and served with a lentil soup called *sambar* and a coconut chutney).

Indian food
When a restaurant gives you an Indian menu it usually lists North Indian preparations. This is also called Punjabi or Mughlai cuisine. *Tandoori* is becoming very popular with the local people of Goa and Kerala; this refers to marinated mutton, chicken or fish barbecued in an earthenware oven and usually served as kebabs or *tikkas*. The main courses of a North Indian meal are rich, with liberal use of cream and nuts. The South Indian restaurants and cafés are usually owned by the Brahmin community and serve pure vegetarian food.

Meal or *thali*
A 'meal' or a *thali* refers to a simple set menu with a fixed price served to everyone. It is usually good, quick, reasonably priced and freshly prepared. A vegetarian meal usually includes vegetables, chapatti, pulses, rice, pickles, yoghurts and sauces, and occasionally a local sweet. A *thali* is a vegetarian meal served on a metal platter, with the individual items in little bowls. Non-vegetarian meals include mutton, chicken or fish dishes.

Ice cream
Well-known brands are Vadilal and Amul, plus international names such as Walls and Baskin-Robbins. Amul also offers Indian ice cream called *kulfis*. Avoid ice cream from hawkers.

WHERE TO EAT
Prices
The cost of a meal can vary considerably, and the following categories are based on the price of an average meal per person, excluding drinks:

* Less than Rs 150
** Rs 150 to Rs 300
*** Rs 300 and above

GOA
Some restaurants close during the off-season (usually between April and September).

Bardez Taluka
After Eight**
Continental restaurant, specialising in fish.
1/274 B, Gauroddo, Calangute. Tel: 22797.

Banyan Tree***
Mainly Thai food, in a beautiful garden setting.
Taj Holiday Village, Sinquerim. Tel: 2276201.

Nilaya Hermitage***
European and Indian set menus, in a pleasant poolside location at one of Goa's well-known boutique hotels.
Arpora Bhati, Baga. Tel: 276793/94. Fax: 276792.

The Plantain Leaf*
Known for its vegetarian Indian dishes.
Near Petrol Pump, Almita 111, Calangute.

Souza Lobo**
Seafood, steaks, sizzlers and Goan curries, served on a shaded terrace.
Calangute Beach. Tel: 2276463.

Panaji
A Ferudara's Horseshoe*
Goan and Portuguese cuisine.
Rua de Qurem, Panaji. Tel: 2431788.

Avanti Hotel *
Air-conditioned restaurant facing Qurem Creek, serving seafood specialities.
Rua de Qurem, Panaji. Tel: 2427179.

Delhi Dubar**
North Indian Continental and Chinese options.
Mahatma Gandhi Road, Panaji. Tel: 2222544.

Geonchin**
Chinese restaurant.
Off Dr D Vaidya Road, Panaji. Tel: 2224405.

Kamat*
A South Indian vegetarian restaurant, specialising in *thali* meals.
No 5, Church square, Panaji. Tel: 2426116.

Quarterdeck**
Overlooks the river and serves Indian, Chinese and Continental food.
D Bandodkar Marg, Panaji. Tel: 2224405.

Riorico**
At the Mandovi Hotel, this restaurant is known for its Goan specialities.
Mandovi Hotel, D Bandodkar Marg, Panaji. Tel: 222451. Email: mandovi@goatelecom.com

Rosaya*
Popular Gujarati vegetarian restaurant with *thali* meals.
18th June Road, Panaji.

Ruchira*
Open-air restaurant with a view of the Mandovi River.
Paris Residency (GTDC), near Secretariat, Panaji. Tel: 227103.

Simply Fish***
Serves good Goan seafood.
Goa Marriot Resort, Miramar. Tel: 437001.

Salcette
Dominick's Shack*
Reputable beach shack with English breakfast, tandoori seafood and Indian curries.
Benaulim Beach. Tel: 2770416.

Jamawar***
Serves a variety of Indian cuisines in attractive surrounds.
The Leela Palace, Cavellossim, Mobor. Tel: 2871234/2871352.

A restaurant perfectly located on the beach in Benaulim

Kentuckee**
A bar and restaurant with a barbecue.
Colva Beach.
Tel: 2788107.

Libia***
Chinese restaurant, with décor to match.
Taj Exotica, Benaulim. Tel: 27771234. Fax: 2771515.

Malibu Beach Café*
Serves Indian and western food in garden setting.
Vasvaddo, Benaulim Beach. Tel: 277181.

Miguel Arcanjo***
Mediterranean food and wines in five-star hotel, with live entertainment.
Taj Exotica, Benaulim. Tel: 27771234. Fax: 2771515.

Patrose*
Family-run beach shack.
Benaulim Beach.

Riverside***
Italian restaurant overlooking River Sal.
The Leela Palace, Cavellossim, Mobor. Tel: 2871234/2871352.

Tito's Beach Shack*
Family-run beach shack.
Benaulim Beach. Tel: 2770053.

KERALA
Cochin
Chariot Fort**
A popular café.
Near Children's Park, Princess Street.

History Restaurant**
Facing the Kochi waterfront, this restaurant has a varied menu reflecting local history.
Brunton Boatyard, Fort Kochi. Tel: 221199.

Kashi*
Popular restaurant with an 'art café' gallery.
Burgher Street. Tel: 221769.

Malabar House Residency*
Heritage hotel serving Italian and Indian food.
Near St Francis Church, Fort Kochi.

Regency*
Wide-ranging menu.
Abad Plaza, MG Road, Ernakulam. Tel: 2381122.

Thiruvananthapuram
Cafe Magnet*
A popular café.
Women's and Children's Hospital, Thycaud.

Kalpakavadi*
Multi-cuisine restaurant.
YMCA Road.

Orion**
Multi-cuisine restaurant.
Hotel Residency Tower, Press Road. Tel: 331661.

Land of Rice and Spice: Coastal Cuisine

Goan food

Goan food has similarities with Indian food elsewhere but makes use of locally grown ingredients such as coconuts, cashews, spices, chillies and *kokum*. Most of the dishes are flavoured with coconut milk, coconut oil, grated coconut flesh or toddy, the sap from the coconut palm. Goans also use *jaggery*, drawn from the palm, for making sweets. Goa depends on the harvest of the sea, and 'fish curry and rice' is a staple food.

Some well-known Goan preparations are *ambottik*, a sour hot curry made of fish but occasionally also of other seafood and meats, *caldeirada* or *caldeen*, a mild seafood dish with or without wine, and *recheido*, fish stuffed with spicy red curry. *Cafrial* is a dry and spicy marinaded chicken or fish, and *xacuti* is pungent curry with coconut rice. *Balchao* is lobster, prawn or fish in a chilli-red tangy curry. *Vindaloo* consists of pork or fish in vinegar, while *sorpotel* is made from diced pork, liver and heart in a thick, spicy sauce which is available in jars. Condiments include *kishmur*, crushed dry shrimp, which are scattered over the main course, and which are eaten with rice, crusty bread rolls or *sana*, steamed rice rolls flavoured with coconut and toddy. The typical sweet of Goa is *bebinca*, made with *jaggery*, eggs, coconut and sugar.

Keralan cuisine

Like Goa, Keralan cooking uses coconut milk, coconut flesh or coconut oil in most dishes. There are regional

variations and differences between the preparations of the Moplah community of Malabari Muslims, the Syrian Christians and the other Malayalees. Arabian influences are obvious in the Moplah cuisine, where dried fruits and nuts are used for gravies and *biryani*. English influences are apparent in the dishes of Syrian Christians.

Typical vegetarian dishes, common to all communities, are *avail*, mixed vegetables in a grated coconut sauce with or without fruits and nuts, *thoren*, vegetables fried or steamed with coconut, mustard and occasionally also green papaya, and *olen*, a coconut-based bean and gourd curry. These are served as accompaniments to rice, with *sambar*, a lentil soup with vegetables, and *rasam*, a flavoured broth.

Fish is a mainstay of the cuisine of Kerala, prepared in coconut curry (*meen pahichadhu*), in chilli-hot curry (*meen vevichatu*) or with sour fruit and chillies (*meen kodampuli*). Mutton, chicken and duck are also popular, with beef common among non-Hindus and pork among non-Muslims.

The various types of bread include *Kerala parathas*, fried wheat flour, pancakes such as *appam*, which is made from rice with a spongy centre, or the crisp *pathiri*. *Puttu* is a popular breakfast made from rice-flour dough. Rice noodles are called *idi-appam*.

Towards the end of the meal, the people of Kerala eat yoghurt-based dishes such as coconut-flavoured curd called *pachadi*. *Payasam* is a popular pudding made from sugared rice or vermicelli.

Opposite: Fish drying on Colva Beach
Above: Fresh food markets are burgeoning with colourful produce

Hotels and Accommodation

Goa and Kerala have a huge variety of accommodation, ranging from family-run guest houses to upmarket resorts. Visitors can expect to find a hotel that suits their needs and their budget in most towns. However, hotels in India suffer from a number of problems that visitors may not have experienced elsewhere, such as dust, mosquitoes and other insects, power cuts and water shortages.

Hotel doorman, Cochin

Price categories

Hotels are graded from one-star to five-star, with categories of four-star and above given by the central government authorities and the lower star classifications by the state government. Hotels are judged on a number of pre-determined standards, from ambience and room size to the qualifications of the staff, services and facilities.

Five-star hotels have extensive facilities, including modern rooms, round-the-clock room service, swimming pools, bar, 24-hour coffee shop and restaurants. Five-star and four-star hotels are a cut below the five-star hotels, while three-star hotels maintain reasonably good standards without the frills of a five-star.

Budget stays

India has many modestly priced hotels. Most of them are located near railway stations, bus stations or near the market, and standards vary considerably. Some can be great value for money, whilst others are downright dirty.

Before booking into a really low-priced hotel, it is important to inspect the rooms to check the standards of cleanliness and to see that everything works.

Hotel in Panaji

Hotel at Bogmalo Beach

Forest lodges

The forest department has lodges and resthouses inside most Indian wildlife reserves. Like the other government guest houses, these too are beautifully located but are rarely well managed and can be difficult to book prior to arrival. The Kerala Tourism Development Corporation manages forest-centred properties in Periyar Tiger Reserve.

Privately owned lodges, resorts and camps are generally located near the entrance to or in peripheral areas of the reserves. These are organised for visitors to the wildlife reserves.

Government guest houses

Government guest houses, such as the Circuit Houses in cities, and the Public Works Department Resthouses, which are located outside the cities and towns, are often grand colonial buildings with equally impressive rooms. Most of them have highly desirable locations, but unfortunately many of them are poorly managed and maintained. Moreover, rooms are generally reserved for government officials, so finding accommodation can be difficult.

Heritage hotels

Buildings built before 1935 that have been opened for visitors are called heritage hotels in India. This is not a homogeneous concept, and it covers a variety of types of accommodation, from five-star palace hotels to bungalows run by the owners.

Accommodation at Terakhol Fort

Goa has just a few heritage hotels, such as Terakhol Fort, Siolim House, Panjim Inn and Panjim Pousada. In Kerala, heritage hotels, such as Ayisha Manzil at Thalasseri and Harivihar at Kozhikode are still partially occupied by their owners. Other old residences, including River Retreat at Cheruthuruthy and Malaabar House Residency, have been converted into hotels. A unique concept in Kerala is the relocation of old wooden houses to new sites, such as beaches and backwaters, to create 'heritage resorts'. Surya Samudra, Somatheeram and Nikki's Nest at Chowara south of Kovalam, and Coconut Lagoon at Kumarakom, are almost entirely comprised of transplanted old wooden buildings.

Plantation houses

It is possible to stay at working plantations, in Munnar, Kumily near Thekkadi (at the entrance to the Periyar Tiger Reserve), and on the way from Thekkadi to Munnar. These plantations all have converted heritage houses, as well as newly built resorts.

Railway retiring rooms

Most railway stations have private rooms and dormitories that are handy for travellers. These are in high demand and are almost always full.

Tourist bungalows

Goa Tourism Development Corporation and Kerala Tourism Development Corporation own and manage tourist bungalows in their respective states. These can be good-value options for travellers, but standards vary considerably.

Upmarket resorts

Resorts at the beaches or hill stations have a special attraction because of their location. Goa has some of India's most famous beach resorts, especially in Salcette Taluka, while Kerala has luxurious resorts along the backwaters, at beaches and at hill resorts. These provide idyllic settings for those who want to indulge in the vast range of facilities available. Such resorts are heavily booked in the winter months from October to March, so early advance reservations are recommended.

CENTRAL BOOKINGS
Abad Plaza
A group of mid-budget hotels in Kerala.
MG Road, Cochin.
Tel: 0484-2381122. www.abadhotels.com
Casino Group of Hotels
This regional group has some of the best upmarket resorts in Kerala, at Cochin, Kumarakom, Kumily, and Marari Beach.
Willingdon Island, Cochin.
Tel: 0484-2668221.
Email: casino@vsnl.com
Leela Palaces and Resorts
A reputed chain with a few well-run hotels, including one of Goa's most famous beach properties.
Sahar, Mumbai.
Tel : 022-56911234.

Treehouse accommodation in the hills of Kerala

Mahindra Holidays and Resorts India Ltd
This resort company has properties at Munnar.
2 Lalithapuram, Gaudiya Mutt Road, Chennai.
Tel: 044-8131170. www.mhril.com
Oberoi Hotels
One of India's best-known hotel chains, operating Trident Hotel in Cochin.
7, Sham Nath Marg, Delhi.
Tel: 011-2389 0505.
www.oberoihotels.com
Park Hyatt Resort and Spa
The Hyatt chain has a spa resort in Goa.
415–417 Antriksh Bhawan, 22 Kasturba Gandhi Marg, New Delhi.
Tel: 011-23358774/5.
Sarovar Park Plaza
Well-represented chain in India, with hotels at Munnar, Thiruvananthapuram and other centres.
42, Mittal Chambers, Nariman Point, Mumbai.
Tel: 022-2350 800.
www.sarovarparkplaza.com
Taj Group of Hotels
One of India's biggest hotel groups, Taj has resorts in Goa and Kerala.
Marine Drive, Ernakulam.
Tel: 0484-2365 161.
www.tajhotels.com
ITC Hotels Limited
This group incorporates Welcomgroup Sheraton, Fortune and Welcomheritage hotels.
Qutab Institutional Area, New Delhi.
Tel : 011-26850242.
www.welcomgroup.com

On Business

India is an important exporter of gems and jewellery, textiles and ready-made garments, marine products, agricultural products, electronics, and engineering goods. The country has entered the new millennium as a leading centre for information technology, with significant software exports and allied services.

Preparing sulphur for shipment, Cochin

Bureaucracy

Despite the reforms introduced by Congress ministers in the 1992 budget, and the present government's promises of a good business environment, bureaucracy still exists in India and you need to be patient with the lengthy procedures involved in government business.

Business dress

Most Indians dress formally for meetings, but the dress code is rarely very rigid. Men should usually wear a smart shirt and trousers, and women should dress equally smartly.

Business etiquette

Business meetings in India usually start with an exchange of introductions and business cards. Social and personal interaction is the norm in India, and most visitors are extended warm hospitality with invitations for lunches and dinners with business associates and their families. The system is, however, formal and hierarchical. Men are addressed as Mr, and women as Mrs or Miss. Academic and military titles, such as doctor or captain, are respected. Indian employees address their seniors as 'sir' or 'madam', and they do not smoke in front of them.

Meetings tend to be lengthy, and Indians usually spend a lot of time over negotiations and discussions. It is a good idea to check things several times, to make certain that you are understood and that others agree with you (Indians rarely argue with foreign visitors, considering it impolite).

Business hours

Most government offices and nationalised banks work from 10am to 6pm on weekdays and shorter hours on Saturdays (some offices are closed on the second and fourth Saturdays of the month). Private establishments have longer hours.

Business services

Most five-star hotels are equipped with business centres, secretarial services, conference halls and messaging services. Telecommunications, internet access and photocopying facilities have improved considerably in India in the last few years, although they do not always compare well with those of more developed countries.

Postal services are inconsistent – excellent in some places and terrible in others – but there are courier services at

Panaji, Thiruvananthapuram, Cochin and Kozhikode.

Food and drink

Hindus rarely eat beef, while Muslims and Jews do not eat pork. Even non-vegetarian Muslims may decline meat at a restaurant if it is not *halal* (prepared according to Islamic law). Most Muslims and some Hindus do not drink alcoholic beverages.

Language

Most executives, business people and high-level government officers speak good English.

The bustling port of Cochin is the scene of much trade and business

Practical Guide

ARRIVING
International
There are international flights to Goa, Thiruvananthapuram, Cochin and Kozhikode, mainly connecting to the Middle East and Southeast Asia. The nearest alternatives are Mumbai (Bombay) for Goa and Chennai for Kerala.

Domestic
Domestic airlines, such as Indian Airlines, Jet Airways and Sahara, connect the gateway cities of Mumbai and Chennai with Goa and Kerala respectively. The overnight train from Mumbai to Madgaon in Goa is a convenient and economical option.

Airports and customs
At the time of writing, visitors are allowed to bring into the country personal items, a camera with five rolls of film, a pair of binoculars, alcoholic drinks up to a maximum of 0.95 litres, 50 cigars or 200 cigarettes, and duty-free gifts up to a maximum value of Rs 600.

Any expensive personal effects or equipment should be registered for re-export. Keep registration numbers handy, especially for laptops, cameras and other expensive equipment, as these are required when you fill in the re-export form. There is a departure tax of Rs 500 for international flights, but some airlines add it to their fare.

Airline offices
Panaji
Air India, *Hotel Fidalgo, 18th June Road, Panaji.*
Tel: 2431100.
Indian Airlines, *Dempo House, D Bandodkar Road, Panaji.*
Tel: 2377821.
Jet Airways, *Sesa Ghor, EDC Complex, Panaji.*
Tel: 2510354.
International Airlines have General Sales Agents at Panaji.

Crossing the river in Goa

Goan car number plate adorned for good luck

Thiruvananthapuram
Air India, *Vellayambalam.*
Tel: 2434837.
Air Lanka, *Vazhuthacaud.*
Tel: 268767.
Air Maldives, *MG Road.*
Tel: 269557.
Gulf Air, *Vellayambalam.*
Tel: 268003 .
British Airways, *Vellayambalam.*
Tel: 266604.
Indian Airlines, *Mascot Square.*
Tel: 2438288.
Oman Airways, *Sasthamangalam.*
Tel: 268950.
Kuwait Airways, *Panavila Jn.*
Tel: 263436.

KLM, *Spencer Jn.*
Tel: 277531.

Cochin
Air India, *MG Road.*
Tel: 2351260.
British Airways, *MG Road.*
Tel: 2364867.
Indian Airlines,
Darbarhall Road.
Tel: 2370242.
Japan Airlines, *MG Road.*
Tel: 2350544.
Jet Airways, *MG Road.*
Tel: 2369729.
Lufthansa, *MG Road.*
Tel: 2370776.

Documentation

Travellers from most countries need a valid passport and visa. You should also carry a set of photocopies in case you lose the originals.

Indian Embassies Abroad
Australia
3–5 Moonah Place, Yarralumla, Canberra.
Canada
10 Springfield Road, Ottawa, KUM IC9.
New Zealand
10th floor, Princess Tower, 180 Molesworth St, Wellington.
UK
India House, Aldwych, London WC2B 4NA.
USA
2107 Massachusetts Avenue, NW, Washington DC 20008.

CLIMATE

Goa and Kerala have a tropical climate, with temperatures ranging from 18°C to 35°C.

Seasons

April to June (summer) is the hottest period and November to February (winter) is the coolest. The coast can become humid in the warm months. The interior hills of Munnar and Periyar Tiger Reserve are more pleasant than the coast in summer, but they can be chilly in winter.

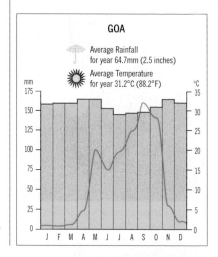

A hot day's labour on the beach at Anjuna

The climate in Kerala is ideal for growing tea

The Monsoon

The southwest monsoon blows in from the Arabian Sea and is condensed by the cooler climes of the Western Ghats, causing torrential rains, lashing waves and powerful winds. There is another wet spell in November and December, which is caused by the retreating monsoon from the eastern Bay of Bengal.

Clothing

Loose-fitting light cottons are most suited to the warm and humid weather of Goa and much of Kerala, but it is a good idea to carry a jacket or a sweater for the evenings, especially if destinations in the Western Ghats, such as Wayanad, Munnar and Periyar, are part of your itinerary. Long-sleeved clothes in light colours provide some protection from mosquitoes.

As a tourist, informal clothes are generally acceptable, but bring some more formal clothes for big hotels, smart restaurants and parties. Wear comfortable shoes and sandals that allow your feet to breathe. Laundry is inexpensive and rarely takes more than 24 hours, but delicate clothes should be washed personally.

COMMUNICATIONS

India is growing into a computer-oriented society and a number of email and internet access centres have appeared

Clothes vendors from Karnataka

It is advisable to wear warmer clothing as the sun goes down

in Goa and Kerala. Most travellers find the poste restante and speedpost services reliable, but the regular postal services are inconsistent.

There are courier services in big cities that guarantee 'desk to desk' delivery, whilst a local courier service, called *angadia*, operates to smaller towns and villages.

CURRENCY

The Indian currency is the rupee, which is divided into units of 100 *paise*. Notes are printed in denominations of Rs 1000, 500, 100, 50, 20 and 10, while coins are minted in Rs 5, 2, 1, 0.50, 0.25, 0.20, 0.10, 0.05 and lower. Indians write Rs 100,000 as Rs 1,00,000 (one *lakh*), with Rs 10 *lakhs* making a *crore*.

Bus station at Idduki

Currency exchange

It is not possible to order rupees in your home country, so you will need to change currency on arrival at the airport. Money exchange is not really a problem in India as banks, hotels and licensed private moneychangers or authorised dealers will happily change dollars or sterling for rupees. Thomas Cook has branches in Goa and Kerala. Collect your encashment certificate, which will help you when you need to reconvert currency. The certificates also help you to pay in rupees at tourist quota counters at railway stations.

Traveller's cheques

Thomas Cook's traveller's cheques are widely accepted for exchange and as payment at hotels, and they are a relatively safe way of carrying money.

Credit cards

Almost all star-category hotels and resorts, expensive restaurants and established shops accept Visa and MasterCard.

Tipping

It is customary to tip 10 per cent at restaurants, Rs 10 to Rs 20 each to hotel porters, and Rs 50 to Rs 100 a day to drivers.

DISABLED TRAVELLERS

Unfortunately, India has limited facilities for disabled visitors. Getting around in a wheelchair on Indian roads, that rarely have pavements, is difficult, few hotels and monuments have ramps for wheelchair access and bathrooms are rarely physically challenged friendly. Hiring a car for the tour is a possible solution as Indian drivers are usually extremely helpful.

HEALTH

Most visitors are immunised against polio, typhoid, tetanus, TB, meningococcal meningitis and Hepatitis A and B before a visit to India.

Take dietary precautions to prevent diarrhoea and intestinal upsets, and make sure that you slap on the sun block, as many travellers suffer sunburn and heatstroke from spending time on the beaches without adequate protection.

Hospitals and medical facilities

Generally, Goa and Kerala have good doctors and there are clinics and hospitals in the cities and in most large towns.

Malaria

Malaria is a serious problem, so see your doctor before leaving home. If you have any symptoms, consult a doctor. Also, protect yourself against mosquito bites by covering yourself completely at night and using repellents.

Keralan food is full of flavour, but beware of potential food-related illnesses

Soaking up the sun on Majorda Beach

Pharmacies

Goa and Kerala have medical stores in cities, large towns and most villages. You will also find medical stores on the highways. The stores usually have local equivalents of most medicines, but carry an emergency supply of essential and prescribed medicines.

LAUNDRY

Laundry services are inexpensive in India. Laundry shops usually do washing, ironing and dry-cleaning but can be rough with your clothes. There may be a small supplement for 'urgent' orders. Laundry services at hotels are usually much more expensive than at the shops.

MAPS

Both Goa Tourism and Kerala Tourism publish tourist-oriented road maps.

MEDIA

In Goa, you will have access to Mumbai or Bangalore editions of national English-language dailies, such as the *Times of India* and *Indian Express,* as well as locally published English dailies like *Gomantak Times, Navhind Times* and the *Herald*. News magazines such as *India Today, The Week* and *Outlook* are also available at newsstands and bookstores.

Almost all hotels have satellite TV in their rooms, with a choice of channels for Indian and international programmes. Besides the foreign channels, you can also access Indian news in English.

PHOTOGRAPHY

Justifiably renowned for their beautiful beaches, lush green waterways, lakes, rivers, waterfalls and hill resorts, Goa and Kerala are extremely photogenic. Besides the magnificent scenery, there are opportunities to photograph dance dramas such as Kathakali, village activities and a huge variety of wildlife.

During the peak tourist season from October to March, Goa and Kerala are generally sunny, except for the occasional shower in the early part of the season, and slow film is ideal for such conditions. You should carry an emergency stock of fast film for low light at dawn and dusk, especially when visiting hill towns such as Munnar, which can become misty in winter, and for the cloudy days of the 'retreating monsoon' in November and early December. Also pack a UV filter and other protection for sunny days.

You will need to cushion your cameras, lenses and accessories when travelling on bumpy highways.

Goa and Kerala are incredibly photogenic!

POST AND FREIGHT

Postal services in India range from excellent to very unreliable. Send letters, postcards and parcels only from the big cities and towns and make sure the covers are franked in your presence at the counter. Important mail should be sent by registered post with a registration receipt and an attached acknowledgement card to be returned signed. Airmail and speed-post services are available at most large post offices. Stamps can be bought at the counters. Poste restante facilities are available at most post offices. Leading courier services like DHL have offices in important destinations like Panaji, Madgaon, Kozhikode, Cochin and Thiruvananthapuram. It is possible to send air-freight from airports like Dabolim, Kozhikode, Cochin and Thiruvananthapuram. The railways and some bus services also take domestic cargo.

SAFETY AND SECURITY

India is fairly safe, and physical assault on foreign travellers is almost unheard of in Goa and Kerala, but it is best to remain alert and avoid out-of-the-way places at night.

Theft

Petty thefts are not uncommon in India. A money belt is a good way to carry handy cash, and an interior pocket is good for small valuables, spare cash and photocopies of documents.

Unattended baggage is an invitation for theft; keep a padlock and chain with you to secure your baggage to any immovable object if you need to leave it for any reason.

On trains, there are wires below the bunks to which you can secure your baggage with a chain and padlock.

TELEPHONES

India has well-developed telecommunications. There are call

The delights of the coastal sky at dusk

A boat on the backwaters brimming with happy daytrippers

booths, called STD-ISD PCOs (public call offices) on all the important highways and in towns, cities and villages that are usually cheaper than calling from hotels for national and international calls. Many PCOs have fax machines. Fax sending charges are based on phone rates with a supplement per page and the PCOs will receive facsimile on your behalf for a per page fee. There are also coin-operated phones that are an inexpensive option for calling locally. Phone cards for cell phones called 'mobile cards' are available in India.

TIME

Indian Standard Time is +5 hours ahead of GMT.

TOILETS

Public toilets are rarely clean in India, and they are almost always of the 'hole in the ground' variety. When travelling, look for hotels and smart restaurants that are likely to have westernised cloakrooms. Keep soap and a stock of tissues handy, and, especially if travelling with children, carry a supply of antiseptic wet wipes.

VOLTAGE

Electric current is 230–240 AC, 50 cycles. Electric power cuts are frequent but usually short-lived. Bring a surge protector to protect any electrical equipment from power fluctuations. Most hotel rooms have both two-pin and three-pin sockets.

WEIGHTS AND MEASURES

India uses the metric system, where distances are in kilometres and weights in grams and kilograms. However, some imperial methods of measurement are still used in places.

ACKNOWLEDGEMENTS

Thomas Cook Publishing wishes to thank the following photographers for the photographs reproduced in this book, to whom the copyright in the photographs belong:

CHAWEEWAN CHUCHUAY/CPA MEDIA: 11, 12, 13, 14b, 20, 29, 40, 42, 46, 47, 54, 57, 73, 74a, 74b, 75, 76, 86b, 91, 93, 94, 98, 102a, 103, 115, 118a, 119, 125, 126, 149, 154a, 158b, 159, 163, 164, 176, 181, 188

RAINER KRACK/CPA MEDIA: 2, 4a, 6, 10, 14a, 15, 16, 17, 18, 19, 21, 22a, 22b, 23, 24, 25, 26, 27, 28, 31, 32, 33, 36, 37, 38, 39, 43, 51, 52b, 53, 56a, 56b, 59, 64, 68, 69, 70a, 70b, 71, 72a, 72b, 79, 80, 84, 86a, 90, 92, 95, 96, 97, 100, 101, 102b, 104, 105, 110, 112, 114, 116, 118b, 120, 124, 127, 130, 134, 140, 144, 148, 150b, 151, 152, 153, 154b, 155, 156, 157, 158a, 160, 162, 165, 166, 169, 170, 171, 172a, 172b, 173, 174, 175, 177, 178, 179, 180, 182, 183, 184, 185, 186, 187, 189

DINESH SHUKLA: 4b, 48a, 48b, 49, 52a, 58a, 58b, 60, 61, 62, 63, 85, 88, 108a, 108b, 109, 117, 122, 128a, 128b, 129, 132, 133, 136a, 136b, 138a, 138b, 139, 150a, 161

Copy-editing: JAN WILTSHIRE

Index: INDEXING SPECIALISTS (UK) LTD

Maps: PC GRAPHICS, SURREY, UK

Proof-reading: CAMBRIDGE PUBLISHING MANAGEMENT LTD and RICHARD HALL

The Author would like to thank the following:

Dr. Venu V, Deputy Secretary, Department of Tourism (Government of India)
T. Balakrishnan of Kerala Tourism
The respective Tourism offices of Goa and Kerala
Dr. Jayathilak, former Managing Director of Kerala Tourism Development Corporation
CP and Faiza Moosa, Thallasseri
George Dominic at Casino Group, Cochin
Anna Kaarina J. Costa, Madgaon.
The staff of Green Gates at Kalpetta and River Retreat at Cheruthuruthy
Claudia and Hari Ajwani, Baga
Rajiv Lal, Munnar
Dr. K. Muraleedhara Menon at Kerala State Electricity.
Lieo and Pramod at Backwoods Camp
Edwin Dias at Resorte Marina Dourada, Arpora
Pioneer Travels in Cochin
My wife Jyoti Mulchandani for her assistance.